ISBN 978-0-260-15473-6
PIBN 10931202

FIFTY-FIRST ANNUAL REPORT

OF THE

𝔐anagers of the 𝔖ociety

FOR THE

𝕽EFORMATION OF 𝕵UVENILE 𝕯ELINQUENTS

TO

THE LEGISLATURE OF THE STATE

AND

THE CORPORATION OF THE CITY OF NEW YORK.

(1875.)

NEW YORK:

6

7

8

9

10

11

FIFTY-FIRST ANNUAL REPORT

OF THE

Managers of the Society

FOR THE

Reformation of Juvenile Delinquents

TO

THE LEGISLATURE OF THE STATE

AND

The Corporation of the City of New York.

(1875.)

NEW YORK:

NATIONAL PRINTING COMPANY, 25 CHAMBERS STREET.

1876.

OFFICERS AND MANAGERS.
1876.

PRESIDENT.
EDGAR KETCHUM.

VICE-PRESIDENTS.

JOHN W. C. LEVERIDGE,   JOHN A. WEEKS,
BENJAMIN B. ATTERBURY,   FREDERICK W. DOWNER,
EDGAR S. VAN WINKLE,   JAMES M. HALSTED.

TREASURER.
NATHANIEL JARVIS, JR.

SECRETARY.
ANDREW WARNER.

MANAGERS.

Term expires 1876.	Term expires 1877.	Term expires 1878.
Charles P. Daly,	James M. Halsted,	Edgar S. Van Winkle,
John A. Weeks,	E. Randolph Robinson,	John J. Townsend,
Augustus R. Macdonough,	Henry Dudley,	Benjamin B. Atterbury,
Andrew Warner,	John W. C. Leveridge,	William M. Prichard,
Edgar Ketchum,	D. Jackson Steward,	Norris Franklin.
Henry M. Alexander,	Nathaniel Jarvis, Jr.,	Alex. McL. Agnew,
Nicholas D. Herder,	Benj. D. Silliman. B'klyn,	James Davis,
Richard M. Hoe,	Elijah H. Kimball,	Cyrus P. Smith, Br'klyn,
Frederick W. Downer,	Robert Kelly,	Henry Q. Hawley, Alb'y
John J. McCook.	Thomas Sullivan, B'klyn.	D. Thomas Vail, Troy.

CLERK OF THE SOCIETY, } CITY OFFICE, BENNETT BUILDING, Cor. Fulton
   W. C. DESMOND,   }   and Nassau Streets, Room 9, 5th Floor.

OFFICERS OF THE HOUSE.

SUPERINTENDENT.
ISRAEL C. JONES.

ASSISTANT SUPERINTENDENTS.
SILAS A. BRUSH,
MARTIN L. ELDRIDGE.

CLERK.
FRANK PERRIN.

PHYSICIAN,   CHAPLAIN.
J. L. COLBY, M.D.   REV. GEORGE H. SMYTH.

OFFICERS OF THE HOUSE.

PRICIPAL OF SCHOOLS.
EDWARD H. HALLOCK.

VICE-PRINCIPAL.
LUTHER S. FEEK.

ASSISTANT TEACHERS.

OSCAR B. M. SHAFFER,
CHARLES W. MANCHESTER,
HELEN PECK,
FRANK EAGER,
ADDIE GRANT,
ELLA M. PURTELL.

PHEBE COLTON,
SUSAN THORPE,
AGNES CARLETON,
GEORGIANA A. SCOTT,
ADA A. BAKER,
HELEN UNDERHILL

STOREKEEPER.
SAMUEL GILDERSLEEVE.

OVERSEER 1ST DIVISION SHOP.
HENRY BRYANT.

OVERSEER 2D DIVISION SHOP.
MICHAEL BURNS.

ENGINEER.
WILLIAM DUGAN.

MATRON.
JULIA O'BRYAN.

ASSISTANT MATRONS.
JULIA BRUSH,   CATHERINE ST. JOHN.

TEACHERS OF GIRLS' SCHOOL.
MARY A. LATHAM,   ALICE STONE.

HOUSE OF REFUGE, RANDALL'S ISLAND.
FERRY FOOT OF 119TH STREET.

STANDING COMMITTEES.

1876.

Executive Committee.

BENJAMIN B. ATTERBURY, NICHOLAS D. HERDER,
CYRUS P. SMITH,   D. JACKSON STEWARD
    NATHANIEL JARVIS, Jr.

Finance Committee.

JOHN A. WEEKS,   J. W. C. LEVERIDGE,
   AUGUSTUS R. MACDONOUGH.

Indenturing Committee.

MORRIS FRANKLIN,   JAMES DAVIS,
FREDERICK W. DOWNER, RICHARD M. HOE,
    HENRY DUDLEY.

School Committee.

EDGAR KETCHUM,   JAMES M. HALSTED,
JOHN J. McCOOK,   ROBERT KELLY,

Law Committee.

WILLIAM M. PRICHARD, EDGAR S. VAN WINKLE,
   E. RANDOLPH ROBINSON.

Library Committee.

D. JACKSON STEWARD, JOHN J. TOWNSEND,
   THOMAS SULLIVAN.

Ladies' Committee.

Mrs. SARAH A. LANKFORD, Mrs. ELIZABETH WOOD,
 " S. M. BERTINE,   " D. B. MILLER,
 " MELISSAE P. DODGE, " MARIANNA M. WOOD,
 " SARAH W. DOWNER, Miss SARAH T. SANDS,
Miss SARAH F. UNDERHILL, Mrs. SOPHIA J. RAY,
Mrs. JANE U. FERRIS,   " MARTHA S. FERRIS,
 " PHEBE J. SAMPSON, " S. M. ADAMS,
   Mrs. ELLEN L. CONGDON.

FIFTY-FIRST ANNUAL REPORT.

To the Honorable the Legislature and to the Corporation of the City of New York:

The Managers of the Society for the Reformation of Juvenile Delinquents in the City of New York, in conformity with the provisions of their act of incorporation, passed March 29, 1824, respectfully

REPORT:

That the whole number of children received into the House of Refuge since its opening in 1825, is..........	16,430
That the number of children in the House on the 1st of January, 1875, was...................................... 789	
That there have been received during the year 1875...... 742	
Making a total of................................. 1,531	
That there have been indentured and discharged during the year 651	
And there remained in the House January 1, 1876....	880

The Superintendent's Statement, hereto annexed, contains all the particulars required by the act referred to, as to the sources from which the inmates of the House have been received, their ages, and the disposition that has been made of them. The statement also shows the parentage of the children, whether native or foreign, as far as we have been able to ascertain.

The receipts for the same period have been:

From the State Comptroller, annual and special appropriations	$78,000 00
From labor	11,729 67
From Board of Education	9,185 42
From theatre licenses	15,383 66
From sale of unused articles	800 00
For board U. S. Prisoners	101 66
Salary of Annie Swindell (ret'd)	20 00
	$115,210 41

The last annual report stated what legal proceedings had been taken to restrain the collection of the license fees required to be paid by proprietors of theatres, and the decision made at the Special Term of the Supreme Court, holding the act of 1872 to be unconstitutional and void, and the unanimous reversal of this decision by the General Term, and the appeal of some of the plaintiffs to the Court of Appeals.

These appeals, with a single exception, were afterward withdrawn, and the actions, with that exception, settled, and licenses for the current year were duly paid for by the parties who had taken those proceedings, and by others, though not by all. For over forty years the Legislature has continued this tax, and the Courts have maintained it as constitutional. And for all this period, public opinion in this country and abroad has approved it. The tax is upon a luxury from which those who supply it derive large revennes, while not they, but those who pay them, bear the tax, and each to a very trifling amount. This has been often shown before the Legislature, which saw that whatever should be remitted must be assumed by the people at large, and therefore it has steadily refused to abolish or reduce the tax. The managers believe this course will still be pursued.

It has often been said in these reports that for the reformation of youthful delinquents, something more than moral precept or human authority must be relied upon; that the word of God is the power given in wisdom and goodness for the government and elevation of mankind; and for the half century the State has committed to this Society the care of these youth, it has found that "The fear of the Lord is the beginning of wisdom;" and has inculcated this truth as fundamental. The rescue from crime of three-fourths of the 16,000 committed here, which the histories show, confirms our belief.

The report of the Chaplain is referred to for particulars of the work done by him and others in giving moral and religious instruction to the inmates. This work is of great importance, and is to be faithfully continued.

The Legislature wisely fixed the limit of age for commitment to this House, at sixteen years; for although there was risk of finding hardened criminals among those who were below it, yet the danger to be encountered from receiving at all those who were older, was too great to incur with safety. It has come to be the opinion of careful observers, that some of the most desperate criminals are to be found between the ages of sixteen and twenty. Their passions have been uncontrolled, and they are reckless of consequences. It was never designed that such as these should be brought into contact with the juvenile offender only beginning a course of wrong doing; but, on the contrary, that they should be wholly separated. Yet, for some years past, through deception practiced on the courts, persons several years older than the limited age, who were deeply depraved, have found their way into the House, where disorder and violence have brought disturbance, with damage to property and danger to human life. They have had places in our schools where there are no manacles or guards or weapons of defence, and have there suddenly sprung upon the teacher, wholly unsuspicious of their purpose. It is to the credit of the great majority that such plots have been formed only by a very few, and that to the loyalty and courage of some who were nigh, the quick discovery and discomfiture of the guilty assailants has been chiefly due.

One of these offenders, convicted on his own confession of an assault with a dangerous weapon, was, in October last, sentenced to the Penitentiary. The House should not be required to receive this class of persons whenever they or their friends choose to swear falsely to their age. The infliction of an alternative sentence, as suggested in the report of the superintendent appended, would prevent the danger to the community occasioned by the liberation of this class of offenders.

The labor of the inmates has, upon the whole, been carried on with such vigor and success during the year as the condition of the labor market permitted. The printing contract has been as useful as was expected. The boys employed under it have been rapidly advanced in the art, and have satisfied the contractor, and earned a good record in the House, bringing them, within a short period, to the degree of merit which has been considered sufficient to justify their discharge, other conditions being favorable.

Other manufactures have been carried on under contracts made with the managers, as will more fully appear in the report of the Superintendent, but the finan cial condition of the country has very sensibly affected them, and the want of a market for the products has lessened the ability of the contractors to pay for labor, so that considerable sums which have been earned, remain as yet unpaid. The prospects for obtaining favorable contracts for the ensuing year are, for the same reason, rendered doubtful.

The Managers are to obtain work for the inmates, if possible, for idleness is baneful both to body and mind; and every effort on their part will be made to procure it, and while doing so to obtain also a fair return for it from those who engage the work.

The labor of the girls is an important contribution toward the common support. They make all the clothes, and do all the washing, ironing, and mending for both departments, which, producing no money (although it saves much) does not appear in the financial account. This year they have also worked under a contract in finishing stockings, as is shown in the report of the Superintendent.

The schools have been conducted through the year without remission and with very good results. The apprehension of the inmates is generally quick, and their advancement from ignorance to knowledge rapid. The teachers have manifested ability and assiduity, holding their classes firmly to order and obedience, so that in no part of the work undertaken in the House is there better evidence of success. The poor children who are brought to us have many of them been grossly neglected and are very illiterate, and find here their first regular and careful instruction. The positive reformatory influence of even the moderate degree of education given here may be learned from the Superintendent's

Report and the tables appended thereto. And for the particulars of the educational work, reference is made to the report of the Principal of schools, which will be found in the Appendix.

It was thought by the Managers that the fiftieth year of their existence as a Society ought to be fitly celebrated, and arrangements were made accordingly, and on the second of June last the celebration was held·at the House on Randall's Island. A statement of the proceedings on that occasion is given at the end· of this annual report. It was gratifying that so many attended on that occasion, and that the approbation was so general on the part of the visitors, of the condition of the House and its inmates, and of its operations generally. Attention is invited to the statement referred to, and especially to the address of the eminent divine who then honored the House with his presence and aid, and to the wise and earnest words of the distinguished statesman who favored it with a letter on that occasion.

The support of the House for the ensuing year is now to be considered. And for all ordinary expenses, other than insurance and improvements, it is estimated there will be necessary.....................$116,000

Insurance and Improvements............   7,500

                                      $123,500.

The probable receipts may be estimated as follows:

From labor of inmates...........:.$30,000
    "   theatre license tax.......... 12,000
    "   Board of Education.......... 9,000
    "   sales of old materials.........   900 —51,900

      Leaving a balance of...................$71,600

Toward which the usual annual appropriation by the State is................$40,000
Unexpended balance from supply bill
of 1875, is...................... 5,000—45,000

    Leaving to be provided for by law, in
    addition to the regular annual appro-
    priation of $40,000 above stated......$26,600

The managers ask therefore of the Legislature, a special appropriation toward the support of the House for
the year 1876, of Twenty-six thousand six hundred dollars, besides the usual annual appropriation stated
above.

Dated, New York, January 1st, 1876.

               EDGAR KETCHUM,
                            President.

ANDREW WARNER, *Secretary.*

Society for the Reformation of Juvenile Delinquents, in Account with Nathl. Jarvis, Jr., Treasurer.

DR.

1875, January 1 to 1876, January 1.		
To Cash for Food and Provisions	$5,516	21
" Salaries	36,061	79
" Clothing	12,846	57
" Fuel	5,695	68
" Furniture	1,920	88
" Buildings and Repairs	2,307	69
" Light	717	19
" Printing Annual Report, &c.	685	30
" Bedding	3,431	71
" Laundry	965	91
" School Supplies	629	82
" City Office, Rent, &c	393	38
" Hospital	166	14
" Traveling Expenses	310	54
" Freight on Supplies	320	94
" Chapel and Sunday School		
" Books and Stationery	196	00
" Postage	142	09
" Stable	117	39
" Funeral Expenses, Inmates	263	40
" Grounds and Gardens	49	00
" Gas and Steam Works	231	45
" 6 Sewing Machines attached to power	859	02
" Telegraph Apparatus	348	00
" U. S. Rev. Stamps	473	72
" Ferry and Boat	18	50
" Interest on Notes Discounted	377	62
" Insurance	445	90
Balance Rent, Dock foot 117 St.	2,590	75
	498	88
	$118,581	47
1875. January 1 — Balance against the Society	2,683	96

CR.

1875, January 1 to 1876, January 1.			
By Balance in Bank January 1, 1875		$677	10
" Cash State Comptroller, Annual Appropriation	$40,000 00		
Balance Special Appropriation, 1874	8,000 00		
On Acc. Special Appropriation, 1875	30,000 00	78,000	00
" Labor of Inmates		11,729	67
" Board of Education		9,185	42
" Theatre Licences		15,383	66
" Articles sold, Bbls., Rags, Iron, &c		800	00
" Board of U. S. Prisoners		101	66
" Salary, Annie Swindell, Returned		20	00
" Balance against the Society		2,683	96
		$118,581	47
1876. January 1, Balance in Bank			$

NATHL. JARVIS, JR., Treasurer.

NEW YORK, January 1, 1876.
We have examined the above account, compared it with the vouchers and found it correct.

J. W. C. LEVERIDGE,
JOHN A. WEEKS,   } Finance Committee.
A. R. MACDONOUGH,

LIBRARY FUND.

Society for the Reformation of Juvenile Delinquents, in Account with Nathl. Jarvis, Jr., Treasurer.

Amount of Fund invested in New York City Stock, $7,000 00.

	RECEIPTS.			PAYMENTS.	
1875, January 1 to 1876, January 1,	Balance with Treasurer........	$718 33	1875, January 1 to 1876, January 1,	Paid Bill for Books by order of Library Committee	$455 36
	Received Interest on Investment	490 00		Balance with Treasurer	752 97
		$1,208 33	January 1.		$1,208 33

1876.
January 1, Balance brought down.........$752 97

New York, January 1, 1876.

We have examined the above account, compared it with the vouchers and found it correct.

NATHL. JARVIS, JR., *Treasurer.*

J. W. C. LEVERIDGE, ⎫ *Finance*
JOHN A. WEEKS, ⎬
A. R. MACDONOUGH, ⎭ *Committee.*

REPORT

LADIES' COMMITTEE FOR 1875.

In presenting our Annual Report, we feel there is cause of thankfulness to the blessed Giver of all our mercies, for His unfailing care over our Institution during the past year.

The number of girls has increased in the past six months from one hundred and nineteen to one hundred and thirty-six. Some of these wayward ones are brought to us from dens of iniquity; others are creatures of circumstances over which they have no control, but all need to be brought to the Saviour of the world, whose blood alone can cleanse each heart from every stain of sin.

We seek not only the reformation and elevation of these, by change of heart and moral suasion, but we aim at making them useful members of the community, by having them taught the simple English branches and domestic duties. They wash for all the inmates of the Institution; make and repair clothes and bedding for between eight and nine hundred boys and girls, and do all the house-work of the girls' building. In addition to this, a certain number are engaged in some kind of contract work, thereby learning a trade. Their general health has been excellent, showing that proper systematic employment conduces to health, and makes them contented and happy. We have reason to believe influences are brought to bear on the girls while in the Refuge which, in many instances, bear fruit during their lifetime. There is decidedly the feeling of a family, rather than that of an Institution. They are, therefore, when thrown on their own resources, better fitted to make their way in the world than those who are simply sheltered, fed, and clothed, as is the case of many institutions of charity.

On inspection, the building has always been found orderly and cleanly, our matron faithfully fulfilling her duties.

In our interviews with the girls they have evinced much interest, and been respectful and attentive; some of them taking special pains to remember from time to time the lesson taught.

May God who is able to make all grace abound, abundantly bless that which was often sown in weakness; and to Him will we ascribe all the praise, for it is ever His due.

On behalf of the Committee,

MARTHA S. FERRIS, *Secretary.*

NEW YORK, December 31st, 1875.

LADIES' COMMITTEE.

MRS. SARAH A. LANKFORD,
" S. M. BERTINE,
" MELISSA P. DODGE,
" D. B. MILLER,
" S. M. ADAMS,
" SARAH W. DOWNER,
" JANE U. FERRIS,

MRS. MARIANA M. WOOD,
" ELIZABETH WOOD,
MISS SARAH F. UNDERHILL,
" SARAH T. SANDS,
MRS. ELLEN L. CONGDON,
" PHEBE J. SAMPSON,
" MARTHA S. FERRIS,

MRS. SOPHIA J. WRAY.

APPENDIX.

SUPERINTENDENT'S REPORT FOR 1875.

To the Board of Managers for the Reformation of Juvenile Delinquents.

GENTLEMEN: Since the opening of the Institution, January 1st, 1825, he whole number of children under its care is 16,430.

Boys	13,091
Girls	3,339
	16,430

The first of January, 1875, the number of inmates was as follows:

White boys	641	
White girls	96	
Colored boys	36	
Colored girls	16	
		789

Were received during 1875:

White boys	588	
White girls	101	
Colored boys	40	
Colored girls	13	
		742
Total in the House during 1875		**1,531**

Were disposed of:

White boys	535	
White girls	78	
Colored boys	24	
Colored girls	14	
		651
		880

Leaving in the House, January 1st, 1876:

White boys......................................	694
White girls.....................................	119
Colored boys	52
Colored girls	15
	880

The following tables give the statistics in the usual form:

TABLE I.—Showing the Sources from whence Children were Received during 1875.

Where From.	White Boys.	White Girls.	Colored Boys.	Colored Girls.	Total.
New York Special and General Sessions	238	16	9	1	264
New York Police Courts...........	42	17	2	3	64
New York Oyer and Terminer....	5	..	..	..	5
United States Court...............	2	..	..	..	2
Kings County	76	7	6	2	91
Queens "	14	1	1	..	16
Westchester County...............	23	..	3	..	26
Rensselaer "	19	4	1	..	24
Albany "	43	8	..	..	51
Orange "	13	2	2	2	19
Columbia "	6	..	..	..	6
Dutchess "	4	4	1	1	10
Ulster "	17	11	2	1	31
Suffolk "	..	..	2	..	2
Richmond "	7	1	1	..	9
Ontario "	..	3	..	..	3
Rockland "	1	1	3	1	6
Chemung "	..	1	..	..	1
Oneida "	..	1	..	..	1
Erie "	..	1	..	..	1
Oswego "	..	1	..	..	1
Schoharie "	1	..	..	..	1
From Juvenile Asylum	1	..	..	..	1
Schenectady County..............	..	1	..	..	1
From Commissioners Charities and Correction, N. Y..................	..	2	..	..	2
Returned by the Courts	61	5	6	..	72
" Themselves	3	2	..	..	5
" by Masters...............	10	12	1	2	25
" by Friends..............	2	..	..	..	2
Total.....................	588	101	40	13	742

TABLE II.—SHOWING THE PARENTAGE OF 638 NEW INMATES RECEIVED
DURING THE YEAR 1875.

American	99	Irish	344
German	72	Jewish	3
African	44	Scotch	7
English	21	Spanish	1
French	8	Mixed	34
Italian	2	Indian	1
Polish	2		
		Total	638

TABLE III.—SHOWING THE AGES OF 638 NEW INMATES RECEIVED
DURING THE YEAR 1875.

1 was	5 years old.	87 were	13 years old.
2 were	6 "	124 "	14 "
2 "	7 "	133 "	15 "
4 "	8 "	94 "	16 "
10 "	9 "	34 "	17
28	10 "	12 "	18
46	11 "	2 "	19
58	12 "	1 "	20

Average age, 13 years, 10 months, 15 days.

TABLE IV.—SHOWING THE OFFENSES OF THOSE RECEIVED DURING
THE YEAR 1875.

Petit larceny	320	Picking pockets	20
Grand larceny	11	Attempt to poison	1
Burglary	30	Truancy	17
Assault and battery	4	Disorderly	135
Manslaughter	3	Arson	1
Vagrancy	96		
		Total	638

TABLE V.—SHOWING THE OFFENSES OF THE CHILDREN COMMITTED TO THE INSTITUTION DURING THE LAST TEN YEARS.

YEAR.	Whole Number Committed.	Committed for Petty Thieving, Vagrancy, Disorderly conduct.	Per Ct.	Committed for Grand Larceny, Burglary, Arson, etc.	Per Ct.	Committed for Crimes agst. the Person.	Per Ct.
			nea'ly		nea'ly		nea'ly
In 1866...	750	655	87	83	11	12	2
" 1867...	682	631	92	42	7	9	1
" 1868...	603	553	92	43	7	7	1
" 1869...	452	418	92	26	6	8	2
" 1870...	406	359	89	44	10	3	1
" 1871...	552	495	90	41·	8	16	2
" 1872...	407	371	91	31	8	5	1
" 1873...	484	402	83	73	15	9	2
" 1874...	636	557	88	70	11	9	1
" 1875...	638	568	89	62	9	8	1
Total ..	5,606	5,019	90	515	9	76	1

TABLE VI.—SHOWING THE CHARACTER OF THE HOMES, SOCIAL CONDITION OF THE FAMILY, HABITS AND ANTECEDENTS OF THE CHILDREN BEFORE COMMITMENT HERE, &C., AS REVEALED IN THE "HOME EXAMINATIONS."

1st. Character and Condition of Homes:

Resided in private houses 67
Resided in tenement houses, and shanties............... 417
Homes comfortably furnished..................... 250
Homes not comfortably furnished..................... 214

2d. Social Condition of the Family:

Fathers living..................... 327
Mothers living..................... 401
Fathers dead 175
Mothers dead..................... 101
Parents separated..................... 35
Step-fathers 43
Step-mothers..................... 37
Temperate fathers and step-fathers 221

Temperate mothers and step-mothers 335
Intemperate fathers and step-fathers.................... 139
Intemperate mothers and step-mothers.................... 79
Parents having property other than household furniture.. 77
Parents having no property other than household furniture 401

3d. Habits and Antecedents of the Children before their commitment
here:

Attended school regularly............................. 134
Attended school irregularly or not at all................ 373
Were habitually employed 162
Were habitually idle................................... 312
Were truants from home and school 312
Were under arrest previous to being sent here............ 221
Had been inmates of other institutions................... 168

TABLE VII.—Showing the Disposition. made of Children sent out
DURING THE YEAR 1875.

	White Boys	White Girls	Colo'd Boys	Colo'd Girls	Total.
Discharged to friends.................	432	37	12	5	486
" to hire	27	7	1	1	36
" by *habeas corpus*..........	2	..	..	..	2
Indentured to farming................	58	..	10	..	68
" to housewifery.............	..	32	..	7	39
" to servant	2	..	..	..	2
" to clerk...................	1	..	..	..	1
Transferred to Alms-house............	1	1	..	1	3
Transferred to Authorities for Criminal Prosecution	3	..	..	..	3
Transferred to Penitentiary under Act of 1873.............................	1	..	..	..	1
Escaped	5	..	..	..	5
Died................................	3	1	1	..	5
Total	535	78	24	14	651

TABLE VIII.—SHOWING THE TIME THOSE DISPOSED OF WERE IN THE HOUSE:

Were in less than 1 month......16 | Were in 21 months............. 6
" 1 month.................17 | " 22 " 11
" 2 " ....13 | " 23 " 9
" 3 " ....12 | " 24 " 6
" 4 " ....18 | " 25 " 2
" 5 " ....24 | " 26 " 4
" 6 " ....22 | " 27 " 2
" 7 " ....25 | " 28 " 4
" 8 " ....24 | " 29 " 3
" 9 " ....27 | " 30 " 4
" 10 " ....21 | " 31 " 2
" 11 " ....23 | " 32 " 3
" 12 " ....103 | " 33 " 5
" 13 " ....35 | " 34 " 5
" 14 " ....51 | " 35 " 1
" 15 " ....36 | " 36 " 1
" 16 " ....25 | " 37 " 3
" 17 " ....21 | " 47 " 1
" 18 " ....26 | " 48 " 1
" 19 " ....20 | " 54 " 1
" 20 " ....23 | Av'age time in house 13 mo's 7 days.

TABLE IX.—SHOWING THE NUMBER OF INMATES WEEKLY.

Date.	Boys.	Girls.	Total.	Date.	Boys.	Girls.	Total.
Jan. 1....	677	112	789	July 2.....	656	122	778
" 8.....	671	112	783	" 9.....	653	119	773
" 15.....	674	113	787	" 16....	649	123	772
" 22....	677	116	793	" 23.....	669	124	792
" 29....	667	117	784	" 30.....	675	117	802
Feb. 5.....	677	118	795	Aug. 6.....	681	130	811
" 12....	677	119	806	" 13.....	688	129	817
" 19.....	693	117	810	" 20.....	691	127	818
" 26....	689	115	804	" 27.....	693	132	825
Mar. 5.....	688	115	803	Sep. 3.....	685	131	816
" 12....	682	115	797	" 10.....	679	132	811
" 19.....	680	114	794	" 17.....	679	132	811
" 26....	672	113	785	" 24.....	677	135	812
Apr. 2.....	670	113	783	Oct. 1.....	687	139	826
" 9.....	659	111	770	" 8.....	687	139	826
" 16.....	650	114	764	" 15.....	696	142	838
" 23.....	652	109	761	" 22.....	697	138	835
" 30.....	647	111	758	" 29.....	708	139	847
May 7.....	644	109	753	Nov. 5.....	707	134	841
" 14.....	640	111	751	" 12.....	717	133	850
" 21.....	641	109	750	" 19.....	726	134	860
" 28.....	650	110	760	" 26.....	725	136	861
Jun. 4.....	648	113	761	Dec. 3.....	738	135	873
" 11.....	638	116	754	" 10.....	738	136	874
" 18.....	644	119	763	" 17.....	733	135	868
" 25.....	651	120	771	" 24.....	737	134	871
				" 31.....	748	133	881
Total....	17,268	2,961	20,229	Total....	18,819	3,500	22,389

Average number...............820.

TABLE X.—Showing the Work Done in the Female Department, Exclusive of the Girls under Contract:

Dresses made	557	Pillow-ticks made		
Aprons "	227	Bed-ticks "	664	
Chemises "	181	Rollers "	124	
Skirts "	143	Boys' pants "	1878	
Cotton shirts made	1,786	" Jackets "	1008	
Flannel " "	1,521	" Caps "	1976	
Pillow cases "	364	" Mittens "	74	
Table cloths "		" Suspenders	989	
Towels "	49	Garments repaired	57,813	
Drawers "	27	Stockings mended	18,407	
Girls under waists made	32	Pieces washed	269541	
Handkerchiefs hemmed	22			

TABLE XI.—Showing the Cost for Support and the Amount of Earnings, per Capita, Annually and Daily:

PROVISIONS.			CLOTHING.			SALARIES.		
Whole Amount.	Per Capita Annually.	Per Capita Daily.	Whole Amount.	Per Capita Annually.	Per Capita Daily.	Whole Amount.	Per Capita Annually.	Per Capita Daily.
$ c. 45,516 21	$ c. m. 55 50 7	c. m. 15 2	$ c. 12,846 57	$ c. m. 15 66 7	c. m. 04 3	$ c. 36,011 79	$ c. m. 43 97 8	c. 12

FUEL AND LIGHT.			BEDDING & FURNITURE.			BOOKS AND STATIONERY FOR SCHOOLS AND CHAPEL.		
Whole Amount.	Per Capita Annually.	Per Capita Daily.	Whole Amount.	Per Capita Annually.	Per Capita Daily.	Whole Amount.	Per Capita Annually.	Per Capita Daily.
$ c. 6,412 87	$ c. 7 82	c. m. 02 2	$ c. 5,352 59	$ c. 6 52	c. m. 01 8	$ c. 825 89	$ c. 1 01	m. 3

ORDINARY REPAIRS.			HOSPITAL.			ALL OTHER EXPENSES NOT INCLUDED IN THE ABOVE.		
Whole Amount.	Per Capita Annually.	Per Capita Daily.	Whole Amount.	Per Capita Annually.	Per Capita Daily.	Whole Amount.	Per Capita Annually.	Per Capita Daily.
$ c. 1 ,412 42	$ c. 1 72	c. m. 00 4	$ c. 166 14	c. m. 20 2	c. 0	$ c. 4,734 47	$ c. m. 5 77 3	

WHOLE EXPENSE.			EARNINGS, AND RECEIV-ED FOR ARTICLES SOLD, BARRELS, RAGS, etc.			NET EXPENSE.		
Whole Amount.	Per Capita Annually.	Per Capita Daily.	Whole Amount.	Per Capita Annually.	Per Capita Daily.	Whole Amount.	Per Capita Annually.	Per Capita Daily.
$ c. 113,328 95	$ c. m. 138 20 6	c. m. 37 9	$ c. 22,511 64	$ c. 27 45	c. m. 7 5	$ c. 90,817 31	$ c. 110 74	c. m. 30 3

In 1874 it was as follows:

WHOLE EXPENSE.			EARNINGS, AND RECEIV-ED FOR ARTICLES SOLD, BARRELS, RAGS, etc.			NET EXPENSE.		
Whole Amount.	Per Capita Annually.	Per Capita Daily.	Whole Amount.	Per Capita Annually.	Per Capita Daily.	Whole Amount.	Per Capita Annually.	Per Capita Daily.
$ c. 104,997 21	$ c. m. 141 88 8	c. m. 38 8	$ c. 42,066 29	$ c. 56 85	c. 16	$ c. 62,930 92	c. m. 85 4	c. m. 23 3

The year opened with 789 inmates—677 boys and 112 girls. This number increased during the year, and we close with 880—746 boys and 134 girls.

The general health has been good. In December a number of cases of measles, of mild type, occurred in both departments. Five deaths occurred during the year—four boys and one girl.

```
The total expense for the year is........................$118,581 47
Expenses for Insurance Interest and Dock Rent...  $3,535 53
Expenses for Extraordinary Repairs and Improve-
    ments........................................  1,716 99
                                                  ————————  $5,252 52

Leaving total Expense for Support....................$113,328 95
Which is Credited by earnings.................... $21,684 24
    "        "      by Board, U. S. Prisoners.......   101 66
    "        "      by Receipts for Articles Sold....  725 74
                                                  ———————— $22,511 64

        Total net Expenses for Support................ $90,817 31
```

The earnings, though much less than former years, have considerably exceeded the estimates made at the beginning of the year. There is due from the contractors, $12,278.06, which is in the way of collection.

The prospects are that the revenue from labor of the inmates will be increased the coming year. The prosperity of the Institution, as a whole, compares favorably with other years.

CONTRACTS.

At the close of the last year, less than fifty boys had employment, except about the Institution. About the first of April a contract was made with the National Printing Co. to employ one-half the boys in the second division for contract, at the printing business. On the first of March, Messrs. J. L. Colby & Co. resumed their work in the first division (not getting their machinery set up, and not being ready on the 15th of February, as expected, on account of the severity of the winter), and increased their contract to embrace two-thirds of the boys in the first division; and Mr. Oliver in the wire shop, at the same time, increased his to take the other third. These two latter were obliged to ask for a reduction in their numbers on the first of July; and the Printing Company made a similar request about the middle of October, neither party being able to employ so many at their respective businesses. The reductions asked for were made; Messrs. Colby & Co. to 125; Mr. Oliver and the Printing Company to 100. There being no demand for the labor at the time, the boys remained idle.

In October a contract was made with Messrs. A. H. & C. B. Alling for 125 boys in the first division, and for 75 girls, to manufacture woolen stockings; and subsequently this firm made another contract to employ 100 more boys in the first division, making their contracts for the boys 225 in all. They are getting to work as fast as practicable, but it is not expected they will have all at work before the first of April.

A contract was made in December with Mr. Robert J. Gemmill, of New York, for 50 boys in the second division to work at umbrellas. He commenced work on the 24th of December, and was not fairly under way at the close of the year.

Messrs. Alling, having doubts of success with the girls, gave the required notice to terminate their contract at the expiration of sixty days, but it is hoped the im provement of the girls will induce the withdrawal of the notice.

There are still upward of 150 boys idle in the second division. The contracts will take up all the boys in the first division (except a few of the very small ones) when they are in full operation.

SYSTEMATIC LABOR NECESSARY.

The experience of the past year satisfies (if there was doubt before) that systematic labor is necessary as a means to the reformation of juvenile delinquents. The happiest, the most contented, and the most hopeful among the boys, were those who were fortunate enough to be chosen for the shops. It is further evident that the form of labor that enlists the mind as well as the hands, is productive of the best reformatory results. Especially is this observed among the boys employed at printing. Not only do they show interest in their work here, but they are hopeful because they see the opportunity, when they are discharged, for earning an honest living —an important matter to them and to the community.

That idleness breeds mischief is not doubted. Several disturbances occurred here during the year, mainly in consequence of it. In some instances violence was used, but fortunately no serious injury was done. The ring-leader in one case was indicted and pleaded guilty to assault with intent to do bodily harm, and was sent to the Penitentiary for three years. Another, an accomplice, was sent to the same prison for six months, under the Act of 1873. A third, having recently come to the house, was returned to court for other disposition, he being beyond the legal age.

Idleness has been the bane of these children. Table
VI. shows that 62 per cent. were habitual idlers. Of
those reported as having regular employment, very
few were engaged in learning any trade or followed
any systematic form of labor. Through idleness their
habits became perverted and their moral and mental
sensibilities blunted. Under no control, they found
their way into the streets to mingle with others
idle and bad as themselves. To reform such and to
train them into industrious and virtuous citizens by
mere precept, without the practical aid of a regular
and systematic form of labor, would be quite as diffi-
cult as to attempt to teach them mathematics without
the aid of figures, or geography without the aid of the
globe and map.

These remarks relate to the moral aspects of the
case. The material side is worthy of notice. While
labor is always to be regarded here chiefly for its
reformatory influence, it has another important consideration as a means for defraying the expenses of the
Institution. Since the establishment of the house, now
fifty-one years, the earnings by the inmates have aver-
aged annually upward of thirty-one per cent. of the
cost of support and care. During the last ten years the
average was nearly 44 per cent.

Another point of the highest importance is, that with
a regular form of labor (and mechanical is preferable),
the boy has the opportunity to earn something for himself to have when he is discharged. The knowledge
that he is participating in the profits of his labor makes
work not a drudgery, but a pleasure, and induces patience and hope, thus preparing the mind in the best
possible way to receive instruction.

The experiment tried in this Institution four years ago—the first of the kind upon an established plan ever tried in any similar Institution—fully demonstrated the importance of this point.

ALTERNATIVE SENTENCES NEEDED IN CERTAIN CASES.

In cases of young offenders sent for crime, who falsely represent their ages under 16 years, and in others under 16 years when admitted, but who are hardened by their criminal practices, whose presence in the House is contaminating, and very little prospect of themselves improving under the discipline, I recommend that alternative sentences be given to such at the time of conviction, proportionate to the crime committed, so that should it be necessary to remove them from the House, on account of their bad influence on the other inmates, and their incorrigibility, they may receive the just punishment due to their offenses.

During the year now past several of this character have been received here, and others were sent; but when it was apparent they were over age, they were rejected and returned to the Court for other disposition. In the case of one committed from Orange County for burglary, he falsely swore his age under 16, and was sent here. He was unruly from the beginning, and gave much trouble. At last he was openly defiant. He admitted that he swore falsely as to his age, to save himself from state prison, and confessed he was upward of 20 years of age and very recently from prison. We were obliged to keep him locked in his room most of the time he was here. He was permitted finally to hire with a bargeman, and so left the Institution no better, and probably worse, than when he came. An alternative sentence would have confined him in prison under merited punishment for his crimes and given protection to the. community. In many cases it is believed that the knowledge that certain punishment awaits them if they refuse to obey the rules here, would restrain their bad conduct and induce obedience, and finally, a complete reformation would follow. The numbers of this incorrigible class are comparatively few, and it is undesirable as well as unprofitable to employ the rigid discipline necessary for their government, while the larger number may be controlled by less severe measures. In the absence of a few incorrigible cases the great majority of the inmates yield a cheerful and willing obedience to the rules under a mild form of discipline, and so make it unnecessary to employ harsh or rigid measures.

I earnestly urge upon the Board the importance of seeking the necessary legislation to accomplish the recommendation here made.

JUVENILE DELINQUENCY MAINLY THE PRODUCT OF NEGLECT, BAD HOMES AND BAD COMPANIONS.

Importance is properly attached to the influence of inherited vicious traits; but I am satisfied that only a small proportion of the young delinquents received here are such from this cause; these, happily few in number, however, tax the wisdom and patience and afford greater discouragements than all the others together, in attempting their reformation. Indeed it may be doubted in some cases, that a reformation can be effected short of the second or third generation. But the large majority of cases are easily traced to the causes named above. That this might be more satisfactorily demonstrated, I prepared, at the beginning of the year, a form of questions, with spaces for answers, relative to the character and condition of the home, the social condition of the family, and the antecedent habits of each child committed here, for the purpose of making a home examination in each case as far as practicable. These forms, with a circular letter explaining the object sought, were sent to the magistrates out of the City of New York, with a request that they would make, or cause to be made, an examination of the homes and return the same with the commitments. This request has been generally complied with. In the cases from New York and vicinity, the examination has been entrusted to Police officer, David Files, who is detailed by the Police Board of commissioners for duty in this Institution. Mr. Files has performed this delicate duty in a very satisfactory manner. In order that the information thus obtained might be preserved in permanent form, a bound volume was made and the reports from the printed sheets, as the examinations were made, have been copied into it. This information has also been of great service to the Indenturing Committee, in determining their decisions in the applications of friends for the release of their children. It is our purpose to continue this home examination, and it is hoped the magistrates will appreciate its importance and make it a point to co-operate with us.

I present the results of these examinations, as far as made in Table VI., to which attention is directed. It shows, with other things, that poverty is closely connected with juvenile delinquency and that intemperance is intimately connected with poverty. In 83 per cent. of the homes visited it was found that the parents possessed no other property than their scanty furniture. Many of the homes were uncomfortably furnished; while in the best there were few attractions to induce the boy or girl to be contented in them. Far the greater number were in tenement houses. These houses were occupied by many families having numerous children, and the rooms were usually untidy, and, in some cases, filthy. From ten to twenty families under one roof were frequently found. One house was occupied by thirty-two families, having, in the aggregate, ninety-six children. In some cases the officer found the parents so much under the influence of drink as to be unable to give intelligent answers to his questions.

Is it any wonder that the children find greater attractions in the streets than in such homes? It is well, in considering the causes of crime, to give large attention to the influences in and surrounding these homes, that it may be ascertained to what extent they contribute to this great evil, and to inquire if, through legislation or otherwise, these hurtful influences and conditions surrounding these unfortunate children may not be corrected.

It is universally acknowledged by parents that bad companions caused their children to go astray, and there is much truth in the statement; but they fail to see that the misfortune came to their children by their neglect.

The evils outcoming from these homes suggest other questions of great importance, but the province of this report does not allow of their discussion here.

JUVENILE DELINQUENCY LARGELY ON THE INCREASE.

At first thought, this might not seem probable, but an examination of the facts reveals the unwelcome truth.

In 1825, and some years before, juvenile delinquency came to engage the thoughtful consideration of some of the eminently benevolent men of that day, and the result was the establishment of this House of Refuge as a practical test of its cure. The act of incorporation at first only embraced the City of New York; but after one year's trial, in 1826, it was made to embrace the criminal children of both sexes in the whole State. This was the only Institution in the State for juvenile offenders for nearly twenty-five years. In 1849 the House of Refuge at Rochester was established, and subsequently, the Juvenile Asylum, the Catholic Protectory, the Hart's Island Industrial School, and the School Ship, all in the City of New York, and several other similar institutions in the State, having for their object the care of this class of children.

The first ten years there were committed to this House, from all parts of the State, 1,678 children, making an annual average of 168. During the twenty-five years prior to the Rochester House, the accommodations here for about four hundred were sufficient for the whole State. The reports of the several institutions for 1874, after fifty years, show that the aggregate number under care at the close of the year was 4,580, an increase of 4,412 for this period, or 2,600 per cent.

During this same period the population of the State increased about 200 per cent., showing that juvenile delinquency has increased in the last fifty years, in proportion to the increase of the population of the State, in the ratio of 13 to 1. This statement does not include children in the care of Children's Aid Societies, Homes for the Friendless, Mission Schools, &c., all of which have to do with this class and tend to diminish its numbers.

That conclusion is hastily drawn that finds this result chargeable to the reformatories established for the cure of this evil. The records of these institutions show most conclusively that they have performed their part well; that 75 per cent. of all committed to their care are reformed and come up to be good members of society. These results commend the efficiency of these institutions in dealing with those under their care.

It is evident from the facts before us that it is impracticable to establish these reformatories upon a sufficient scale to insure protection to the community against this evil. The outlay of a few thousand dollars at the outset was found sufficient to carry on the work. As the evil increased larger sums were appropriated, until now more than a million are required to sustain these institutions. How much more is required to increase their number and power to successfully grapple with this evil is not easily estimated. Where, then, is the remedy? To this question I have but one answer: reform the homes, the sources of this evil, and make it obligatory on the parents to send their children to school and look after them when out of school, and so keep them from mischief; and there can be little doubt, in the presence of the foregoing facts, that a large proportion of juvenile delinquency will disappear.

DIFFICULTY IN FINDING PROPER PLACES.

The first thirty years the demand for boys' help on the farms in this and the adjacent States, and on whaling-voyages, was sufficient to take all that were suitable for these occupations. Occasionally a boy was apprenticed to learn some mechanical trade.

These several occupations took up about 86 per cent, of the inmates of the Refuge during the above period, the annual average number being then about 250 boys and girls. The next ten years, 1855 to 1865, the number of commitments increased, and the annual average was about 350. The places offering were for about 60 per cent. of the whole number.

The last ten years, 1865 to 1875, the number of commitments nearly doubled those of the preceding decade. and only about 26 per cent. could be placed at any of these occupations. Thus it is seen that only about one quarter was apprenticed during the last ten years and there is no probability that the opportunity to find places out of the city will be any better in the future. Probably about 50 per cent. of the boys and girls sent here these later years (the class as a whole is of a higher grade than formerly), can safely be returned to their homes. This class is made up of those who have fair homes, but who, from carelessness or thoughtlessness of their parents, have been allowed too great freedom at night, and who unfortunately have been drawn aside by evil companions. A few months' detention and discipline generally serves to correct their habits, and what is more important, brings forcibly to the parents' mind the necessity of guarding their children, and so save them from greater evils.

This leaves about 25 per cent. without places, and it is to this class that particular attention is directed. This House of Refuge seems to be charged with the responsibility of starting this 25 per cent. of boys and girls in life, and befriending them until they come to have experience and ability to care for themselves. For such I recommend that they be detained in the House for a longer period, not less than three years, and that they be taught thoroughly some trade, and have an opportunity to earn for themselves a fit-out of clothing and some money for a start when they are discharged.

ISRAEL C. JONES,

Superintendent.

NEW YORK HOUSE OF REFUGE,
RANDALL'S ISLAND, *Dec.* 31, 1875.

————:0:————

REPORT OF THE CHAPLAIN.

To the Managers of the Society for the Reformation of Juvenile Delinquents :

GENTLEMEN: It is with gratitude to God the chaplain records another year's pleasant, and he trusts, profitable labor for the reformation and well-being of the children committed to the House of Refuge.

Throughout the year every circumstance has favored his work. The children have evinced a grateful appreciation of his efforts to do them good, or as they express it, to *make* them good. In this the officers, one and all, have most heartily co-operated with him. The frequent presence, hearty sympathy and personal services of members of the Board in addressing, counseling and cheering the children, as well as stimulating and strengthening the teachers, have aided largely in whatever good has been done. The opportunities have been many and favorable for instructing and helping these children to reform.

The longer the writer is engaged in this work, the deeper his interest becomes. To study these children individually and collectively; to find out the predisposing causes of their delinquencies; to learn their wants, discover their weaknesses, and so adapt the healing, helping remedies of the Gospel to them as to be effective in their reformation, has been his aim; for he is profoundly impressed with the absolute necessity of reaching the moral nature of these children before any thorough or permanent reformation can be effected.

Wholesome restraint, suitable industry, education, social and kindly influences, are all important and essential agencies in emancipating the soul from the thraldom of animal passions and appetites; yet these do not go deep enough to eradicate the moral diseases of depraved humanity. Comparatively strong intellects are occasionally found in very wicked criminals, while weak intellects are not unfrequently associated with strong moral natures.

The *root* of all crime is found in the weakness, corruption or perversion of the moral nature; hence, until the·remedy is effectually applied here no true reformation is produced.

The same course of religious teaching pursued in the House during the fifty years of its history still obtains, and cannot be better expressed than in the language of the former Chaplain, Rev. Dr. Pierce: "We have maintained inviolably the true position of a public institution upon the disputed points among the Christian denominations, interpreting the teaching of our common Scriptures upon those fundamental truths lying at the foundation of piety and wholesome morals which all hold without serious difference of sentiment. . . . . To introduce sectarian instruction into the Refuge would destroy the fundamental idea upon which it is based, and introduce among its inmates perplexing and hurtful discussions and controversies."

Clergymen of all the Christian denominations have, from time to time, been cordially welcomed to the pulpit of the house to preach to the inmates, the only limitation being that nothing sectarian should be taught. Besides, whenever a child or his friends desire the personal instruction of his own minister, or the sacred services of his own particular church, as in the case of a hospital subject dangerously ill, we promptly send for the chosen administrator, and cheerfully afford every facility for discharging the solemn service.

The close attention, the deep interest, at times the tearful impression seen among the children in the chapel service on the Sabbath, have touched tenderly the hearts of the visitors—of all religious denominations—who frequent these much enjoyed services, and who leave often breathing a prayer of gratitude that there is such an institution for the neglected, tempted children of the street.

The scripture lessons prepared by the American Sunday School Union, and now used almost universally by the Sunday School world, are adopted, being considered free from any sectarian bias, for Sabbath-school instruction. These are taught by the trained and experienced daily teachers of the children, aided by Managers Ketchum and Herder, whose presence is most inspiriting to the teachers and gratefully profitable to the taught, also Mr. Hadden, member of the Young Men's Christian Association.

In passing from school to school of our three divisions—namely, two male and one female—addressing each, the Chaplain finds one of his best opportunities for good. Also in his visits to the evening schools during the week, after going from class to class, and then at the close addressing each school collectively on educational or moral topics and concluding with prayer.

The Wednesday evening lecture and social worship for the officers is always well attended and greatly appreciated by all, as it is believed to be of great good indirectly to the children.

From the confining nature of their duties, the officers are in a measure debarred from the regular ministrations of their respective churches, and it is all important to have the influence of the Gospel to keep the largest sympathies of the heart awake to the wants and well-being of the children, as it is needful to seek together the divine blessing upon our common work —a work, the success of which, as has been well said, depends more upon the individual qualifications of the persons engaged in it, the wisdom and enthusiasm with which it is prosecuted, than upon any particular system of reform or peculiar machinery applied. The demand of the age is for skilled labor in all departments of life, especially in those that relate directly to the well-being of man. Hence the schools for the training of teachers, cooks, nurses; lay colleges for Christian workers, Sabbath school institutes; medical associations. If the man who heals the body requires a thorough training and long experience, much more he who would eradicate the diseases of the mind, and deal with it in all the complex windings of its mysterious nature.

In no department of life is natural adaptation and special training more needed than in the reformation of juvenile delinquents. The seed sown in these youthful hearts—often very barren soil—by sermons, lecture lessons, personal conversations, daily devotions, kindly admonitions, we are not permitted to see ripen except in comparatively few cases; for when a boy has given evidence of reformation he is dismissed on the first opportunity that offers him a proper home and legitimate employment. But from time to time we do see that the seed cast upon the water, is not lost.

The well-to-do farmer comes to cheer the boys and express his gratitude to the House where he was an inmate more than forty years ago. The lad that went from the Refuge on a whaling voyage turns up many years after, master and owner of his vessel. A promising law firm, two hours ride from this Island, is composed of two of our graduates, who afterwards took their diplomas from the best college of their State. "The hero of Melville's South-Sea fiction—Omoo and Typee—was once a boy of the Refuge, and is still living. He is now a worthy member of the Episcopal church in a New Jersey city. With his rector he lately dined at the house."*

A list of the faithful, efficient officers in the house, taken from the boys and girls for the last fifty years, would make a roll of honor alike creditable to the Institution and its wards. Alas! all do not turn out well, but if twelve thousand of the sixteen thousand who have come under the care of the Refuge are saved from a life of vice and set forth on a life of virtue, as the records show, then is it worth while " to labor and to wait " for even greater success.

When we think of the many others whom these 12,000 might have corrupted had they gone on in their criminal career, of the sorrow to their friends, suffering to themselves, and the evils entailed upon the State, we cannot easily over-estimate the wisdom and economy that seek to check crime and pauperism in their early stages.

The Prison Association of New York has given to the public some significant and suggestive facts in the history of a certain criminal family traced through six generations, and for a period of 75 years. The family is said to have numbered 1,200 persons. The paupers of it had received an aggregate of 2,150 years out-door relief and 150 years of Almshouse life. The criminals of this family received 140 years' imprisonment, and the entire family cost the community over $1,000,000. Had the woman from whom this progeny sprang been reformed in her youth, probably little account would have been made of it, just as little estimate is placed by some on the work of the reformatory. Little note is

---

* Appleton's Journal, March, 1871.

made of the *ounce* of *prevention*, but by and by the *pound* of *cure* startles the people, as it taxes their purse and exhausts their patience. Some one has said it would be wise economy for the State to board every criminal at the Fifth Avenue Hotel if that would put a stop to crime. Be that as it may, no one will doubt that if crime and pauperism can be prevented, the remedy must be applied to the children, and the earlier the better. It would be a great step gained in advance if the measures adopted were such as would reach the child before the child reaches the Reformatory.

The most effectual preventive would begin at the nursery. Cruelty to animals is bad, but cruelty to infants is monstrous, and the humane law that steps in to shield the brute should not be less humane in stepping in to save the boy. Were Mr. Bergh to stand by while some untoward teamster beat and cut his horse, and then come with bandages for the poor animal, he might be esteemed kind, but would certainly be thought careless; and when the community stand by and see a child battered and bruised into a criminal on the street, and come along only to poultice the wounds it might have prevented, it is a day too late with its remedy. The child, if ever healed, will be scarred through life, the stigma of crime will be upon him, the poison of crime will be in him. It was Ex-Gov. Seymour who said in his letter prepared for the Semi-Centennial of this Institution— "The conviction grows * * * that the existence of crime in any community is proof of the guilt of the whole community."

What is the remedy? Purification of vicious neigh-

borhoods, renovation of impure homes,* or the early removal of the child from their damaging influence. Let
there be some moral vaccination applied.

In our immediate work some encouraging items of
the past year may be noted. 1. The community is becoming more familiar with the aims and operations of
the House, and have accordingly a higher appreciation
of its worth and a more intelligent sympathy with its
work. Some visitors are agreeably surprised to find, instead of a prison, a home of healthy, happy children, in
respectful and friendly association with the officers. 2.
The parents for the most part have a very grateful
sense of the care and kindness exercised over their
children. 3. The better part of the inmates are in
hearty accord with the efforts put forth for their welfare.

Visits are often made to the House years after their
departure from it by former inmates, who have most
grateful recollections of the officers and teachers that
sought and labored for their good. Only two evenings
since one such came into the Superintendent's office.
He was of respectable appearance, and a well doing
young man. He had with him a ragged, wretched
looking boy whom he found in want and without
friends. He had brought this child up, after caring
for him as for a brother, to have him placed in the
House that had done so much for him. His expres-

---

* Dr. Elisha Harris— on sources of crime before the Assembly
Committee, and after this report was in type—said, * * * * "the
young criminals nearly all came from the worst tenement houses in the
city. He thought there should be a law regulating the number of families in a house. In Glasgow the authorities tried this plan, and also that
of keeping tenement houses clean, and the result was as follows: Total
crimes reported in 1867—16,899: Total crimes reported in 1873—7,869."

sions of appreciation and gratitude, as well as his
tender solicitude for this unfortunate boy, were very
affecting. 4. It is no uncommon occurrence to see
genteel young men bring their younger brothers to
the House that they say and feel saved themselves
from ruin. In like manner, grown up and married women bring their younger sisters, and the scenes witness-
ed on those occasions at times compel our tears to
mingle with theirs. 5. The Chaplain scarcely ever
visits the city that one or more of the discharged boys
do not meet him with the most friendly greeting in the
streets, to tell him how well they are now doing, and to
send messages of affection to the teachers and officers
of the Refuge. Many are the individual cases of reform
which come to his knowledge among these children,
and many and noble are the struggles made by
them against inborn evil tendencies and inbred evil
habits.

We are under renewed obligations to the Bible
Society for its generous supply of Bibles to the Institution, and also to the Reformed Church of Harlem
for its liberal donation of *The Illustrated Christian
Weekly*, a paper greatly appreciated by officers and
inmates.

To the constant, earnest labors of the Managers,
so generously expended for the welfare of the children, the Chaplain is indebted for valuable assistance, noble example and inciting inspiration in his
work.

To the mature experience of the Superintendent and
his assistants, the Principal of Schools and his excellent
corps of teachers; to our esteemed Matron and asso-
ciates in their more intimate acquaintance with the

wants of the children, the Chaplain gratefully acknowledges his indebtedness. The pleasant relations enjoyed by him with every officer in the House, the friendly regard of the children, their reformation while here, and their prosperity in after life, are among the most valued rewards of his labor.

The Chaplain knows no distinction of faith among these unfortunate children, but seeks earnestly, by the Divine help to lead them, one and all, up to Him who came " to seek and to save the lost."

Respectfully submitted,

GEORGE H. SMYTH,
Chaplain.

HOUSE OF REFUGE,
Randall's Island, January 1, 1876.

——:o:——

PHYSICIAN'S REPORT.

To the Board of Managers of the Society for the Reformation of Juvenile Delinquents.

GENTLEMEN: Your physician respectfully reports: The whole number of inmates in the Refuge during the year has been 1,531   The whole number admitted to the hospital, in both departments, has been 192.   We have had five deaths among the inmates during the year, viz, John Brennan died Feb. 13, of Apoplexy; Octavius Barker died March 30, of Diphtheria; Thomas Smith died Sept. 20, of Typhoid Pneumonia; and Mary Fleming died July 3, of Pneumonia; William Thurbey, Dec. 25, Pericarditis. Nothing has occurred in the medical department of the Refuge since my last report worthy of special note. The children have enjoyed, for the most part, uninterrupted health during the year. The diseases which we have been called upon to treat, with few exceptions, have been of a mild character, requiring but little medication.

I have so frequently called attention in former reports to the causes which we believe have contributed so much to the health and comfort of the children in this Institution, that I deem it unnecessary to revert to them again at this time.

The House is free from Ophthalmia. No epidemic or contagious diseases, with the exception of measles, has visited us during the year. This made its appearance in November among the boys of the first division, and among the girls, where it has been mainly confined; we have had in all 42 cases. Extra care exercised over these cases and good nursing have no doubt contributed largely in preventing the usual organic complications and sequences of measles liable to take place from exposure, particularly at this season of the year; so that very little medication has been required, and the disease has now entirely disappeared from the House. The year closes with no sickness in the Hospital.

JOHN L. COLBY, *Physician.*

REPORT OF THE LIBRARIAN.

To the Board of Managers of the Society for the Reformation of Juvenile Delinquents:

GENTLEMEN : To the different departments of the library there has, during the past year, been a gradual addition of choice and meritorious works. The books chosen are selected with great care, and with a view to assist in the work of education and reformation. The instructors and all the other employees of the Institution, are, at the officers and teachers' library, furnished with those works which note the progress of the age, and in which is recorded the advancement in literature and science.

For the libraries of the boys and girls, the recent selections are of a moral tone, containing principles of duty and sentiments of honor, and are well calculated to incite the peruser to emulate worthy and exalted characters, and to begin a course of self-restraint and discipline. By such additions, the library has, by degrees, been increasing in value, and is now a depository suitable to the condition of the inmates and sufficient for their present need.

In the main library used by the employees, there are 1,502 volumes, and in the cases for the boys and girls, there are 2,584 volumes, amounting in all the departments to 4,086 works. The distribution of one hundred and twenty-five copies of the *Youth's Companion* has been continued during the year, and forty-four copies of the *Illustrated Christian Weekly* have again been given to the boys of the First Division by the Sabbath School of the First Reformed Church of Harlem. The benefit derived from the library by the inmates has been commensurate with the advantages it has offered ; and its good effect, in nearly all cases, is seen in their intellectual development and moral bearing.

Respectfully submitted,

LUTHER S. FEEK.

Jan. 1st, 1875.

REPORT OF THE PRINCIPAL OF SCHOOLS.

To the Managers of the Society for the Reformation of Juvenile Delinquents:

GENTLEMEN: I have the honor to submit the following statistics as the Report of the Schools of this Institution for the year ending December 31st, 1875.

On the 1st of January, 1875, there were in the schools 789 children namely, 677 boys and 112 girls. Since then we have received 625 boys and 114 girls; making the total number under instruction during the year......................1,531

Those that were received were entered in divisions, as follows :

Boys in First Division.......................	308
" Second Division.....................	320
Girls in First and Second Divisions.........	114
	742

And were classified :

IN READING.

	BOYS.		GIRLS
	1st Div.	2d Div.	1st & 2d Div.
Primer...............................	127	51	53
1st Reader.........................	76	66	29
2d "	47	92	8
3d "	36	64	14
4th	22	47	10
	308	320	114

In Arithmetic.

Commencing Addition..............	202	123	72
" Subtraction..........	12	51	9
" Multiplication........	40	39	11
" Division..............	30	50	9
" Compound Numbers.	14	40	8
" Fractions............	10	17	5
	308	320	114

PROMOTIONS.

In Reading.

	BOYS.		GIRLS.
	1st Div.	2d Div.	1st & 2d Div.
To 1st Reader......................	139	99	49
" 2d "	155	133	46
" 3d "	153	127	46
" 4th "	133	127	57
" 5th "	129	119	47

In Arithmetic.

To Subtraction....................	154	105	47
" Multiplication............,....	150	131	46
" Division.................'.........	154	155	45
" Denominate Numbers...........	159	126	45
" Fractions......................:......	73	98	37
" Decimals.......................	43	66	17
" Miscellaneous Arithmetic.......	39	55	6

There are now in the schools 880 children, namely:

Boys in 1st Division.............................	423
" 2d Divirion.............................	323
Girls in 1st and 2d Divisions....................	134
	880

PRESENT STANDING.

In Reading.

	BOYS.		GIRLS.
	1st Div.	2d Div.	1st & 2d Divs.
Primer.........................	45	6	13
1st Reader.........................	80	30	10
2d "	85	73	22
3d "	80	58	47
4th "	74	62	22
5th "	59	94	20
	423	323	134

In Arithmetic.

In Addition	85	36	45
" Subtraction	40	33	15
" Multiplication	85	40	13
" Division	80	58	19
" Denominate Numbers	74	62	22
" Fractions	33	63	12
" Percentage	21	19	8
" Miscellaneous Arithmetic	5	12	0
	423	323	134

In Other Studies.

	BOYS.		GIRLS.
	1st Div.	2d Div.	1st & 2d Divs
Mental Arithmetic	298	214	61
Geography	253	156	42
Writing in Book	295	287	74
Slates	128	36	60

DISCHARGES.

Whole number discharged 651, namely:

Boys in 1st Division	284
" 2d "	275
Girls in 1st and 2d Divs	92
	651

STANDING WHEN DISCHARGED.

In Reading.

	BOYS.		GIRLS.
	1st Div.	2d Div.	1st & 2d Divs.
In 1st Reader	31	13	37
" 2d "	52	16	7
" 3d "	86	55	15
" 4th	85	90	17
" 5th	30	101	16
	284	275	92

In Arithmetic.

Addition	42	12	35
Subtraction	12	15	9
Multiplication	31	19	15
Division	76	47	14
Denominate Numbers	45	101	8
Fractions	33	21	7
Percentage	10	20	4
Miscellaneous Exercises	35	40	0
	284	275	92

In Other Studies.

In Geography	78	71	19
" Mental Arithmetic	123	282	33
Writing in Books	230	245	58
Slates	54	27	44

In summing up the labors of the year, I have the impression that the profounder mysteries of our work are only approximately fathomed at the best, and then only, after a long and varied experience. It were possible to consider it as a governmental measure only, full of wisdom and power in execution, yet evincing no feeling of pity or sympathy for the unfortunate subjects of our care. If so, we should perform our labors as a matter of duty, or in obedience to some behest of necessity. The Gospel informs us that our Saviour came in our nature, became our brother in condition and experience, that He might minister to our wants and assure us of Heaven's infinite pity upon us, and desire for our salvation. Hence the sympathy of Christ is one of the great attractions of His character and one of the chief elements of His power. It certainly becomes us to exercise this element in a large degree in our labors here.

Sympathy is one of the latent forces of our being. We cannot philosophize upon it, yet all confess its power. It sometimes flashes along every line of the soul, conquering minds when every other device has failed. Our life here is full of illustrations of this fact.

There are minds, however, that sympathy, in common with all other efforts, fails to reach. They are found among the older boys. One thing, it seems to me, is established beyond question. A boy's chance for reformation begins to wane at fifteen years of age, and at seventeen his case is almost hopeless.

Unless a separate department can be organized for boys at that age, and they be put under special training, and under a more rigorous discipline than the Institution contemplates as at present organized, it were far better to reject them, as their presence and example are ruinous to the rest.

They interrupt a work which both parents and pupils seem to have appreciated more during the past year than ever before, if the constant daily expressions of both parties are any criterion.

It gives me great pleasure to speak of the general efficiency and commendable unity of effort now manifest in my class teachers.

As at present organized, we are prepared for efficient school work.

Permit me especially to speak of Mr. Luther S. Feek my vice-principal, for general efficiency and special fitness for the duties of his position.

Allow me to express my gratitude to the School Committee for their expressions of sympathy and kindly assistance during the year.

I pause in this writing, while I hold in contemplation

the eight hundred souls before me with all their necessities and wants.   Each has a separate nature with special personal powers which he cannot alienate, and which we cannot take from him; poisoned, perhaps, at the fountain, tarnished by voluntary alliance with evil, yet possessing numerous inherent and wondrous qualities that live even though the soul descends to the deepest infamy.

Each one is struggling on towards the judgment with such interests about him that were he to be reformed in heart and life, it would cause a thrill of emotion in all the realms of heaven, for there is joy in the presence of angels over one sinner that repenteth.

Let us consecrate ourselves anew to the work, and reap the reward;

> Yea, such reward
> As awaiteth those who the young shall turn
> To righteousness; a name above the stars
> That in the cloudless firmament of God
> Forever shines.

E. H. HALLOCK,
Principal.

Dec. 31st, 1875.

REPORT

OF THE

Semi-Centennial Anniversary Meeting

OF THE SOCIETY FOR THE

REFORMATION OF JUVENILE DELINQUENTS.

At a meeting of the Board of Managers on 5th June, 1874, it was, on motion of Mr. Alexander—

Resolved, That the Managers of the Society will celebrate its Semi-Centennial Anniversary with appropriate ceremonies, and that a Committee be appointed to report suitable arrangements for the same.

The following gentlemen were appointed such Committee, viz.:

The President, Mr. Van Winkle, Mr. Warner, Mr. Leveridge, Mr. Silliman, and Mr. Kelly.

It was subsequently determined that the day for the celebration should be Wednesday, the 2d June, 1875, and that Rev. John Hall, D.D., and Hon. Horatio Seymour should be invited to address the assemblies of the morning and afternoon.

Rev. Dr. Hall accepted the invitation, and Gov. Seymour, being unable to do so, promised a letter expressing some things he desired to say.

The children were prepared for their part in the songs for the occasion by Prof. S. Lasar, of Brooklyn. Three of them were selected from Luther, Bonar, and Lyte. The other was written for the occasion.

The following invitation was issued to many official persons and clergymen, and to many other gentlemen and ladies.

NEW YORK, MAY 20th, 1875.

The present year commemorates the Semi-Centennial Anniversary of the founding of the SOCIETY FOR THE REFORMATION OF JUVENILE DELINQUENTS, in the City of New York, and the Managers deeming that the occasion calls for some public recognition of the power of Christian effort in behalf of the neglected children of our City and State, respectfully invite you to unite with them in such exercises as seem appropriate to the occasion, and ask you to be present at the House of Refuge, Randall's, Island, on Wednesday, the second day of June next, at 10½ o'clock A. M. to join with them in commemorating this period in their history.

In behalf of the Board,

> EDGAR KETCHUM,
> ANDREW WARNER,
> EDGAR S. VAN WINKLE,
> ROBERT KELLY,
> BENJAMIN D. SILLIMAN,
> J. W. C. LEVERIDGE

Committee.

On the appointed day, the weather was favorable, and all the inmates were assembled in the chapel, and ample space was left for the visitors who came over from Harlem and the lower part of the city, and also from Brooklyn.

Among those present were Hon. George G. Reynolds, Judge of the City Court, Brooklyn; Hon. Gilbert M Speir, Justice of Superior Court; Hon. Charles P. Daly, Chief Justice; and Hon. Richard L. Larremore, Justice. of the Court of Common Pleas; and Hon. John J. Armstrong, County Judge, Queens County; Col. Pearsall, of Governor Tilden's staff; Hon. Daniel P. Ingraham, late and for many years a Justice of the Supreme Court; Police Justices Kilbreth, Otterbourg, and Wheeler, of N. Y.

And of the clergy Rev. Cyrus D. Foss, D.D.; Rev. E. H. Gillett, D.D.; Rev. B. K. Peirce, D.D., of Boston, formerly Chaplain of the House; Rev. Henry Mandevill, D.D.; Rev. E. D. Murphy, Rev. James Ramsay, Rev. Thomas H. Birch, A. R. Wetmore, Esq., President of the New York Juvenile Asylum; and other gentlemen and ladies to the number of about four hundred

Also of the managers, the President and Messrs Van Winkle, Warner, Leveridge, Sullivan, Atterbury, Davis, Hoe, Halsted, Cyrus P. Smith, Jarvis, Dudley, Daly and Kelly.

The exercises were opened by the reading of the Scriptures by the Rev. B. K. Peirce, D.D., of Boston, who was followed by the Rev. George H. Smyth, the Chaplain of the House, in prayer.

Prof. Lasar, accompanied by four trumpets from the orchestra of Theodore Thomas, led the boys and girls in singing the following hymn:

THE CHIMES OF LONG AGO.

BY MRS. SUSAN K. BOURNE, OF PATERSON, N. J.

Tune—*Lauriger Horatius.*

Ring, sweet chimes of long ago,
   All our story telling;
Sing the thoughts that in us glow,
   Every bosom swelling:
     Sing the tale of noble deed,
      Every barrier leaping;
     Sing the sowing of the seed,
      We with joy are reaping!

Softly sweet your echo rolls,
 Mournful cadence keeping;
Telling of those noble souls,
 Who in death are sleeping :
  Be our lives their monument,
   In our hearts their glory—
  Lives on high endeavor bent,
   Saved from crime's dark story.

Fifty years have passed away,
 Since the first seed-sowing;
Fair the harvest waves to-day,
 In the sunshine growing :
  Ring—sweet chimes of long ago!
  Send the echoes flying,
  Till the notes of crime and woe,
   Sink in silence dying.

Joyously the happy years
 Golden sheaves have treasured :
Saved from vice and sorrow's tears,
 Lives for good unmeasured.
  Ring—sweet chimes of long ago!
 . All our story telling;
  Sing the thoughts that in us glow,
   Every bosom swelling.

May we all with heart and hand,
 Precious lessons learning,
Join the march of virtue's band,
 Richest honors earning.
  Ring—sweet chimes of long ago!
  Send the echoes flying, .
  Till the notes of crime and woe,
   Sink in silence dying.

The President of the Society, Mr. Edgar Ketchum,
then made the opening address as follows:

ADDRESS BY THE PRESIDENT.

Ladies and Gentlemen, honored visitors and friends:

It was Bedford Jail that was the birth-place alike of the Pilgrim's Progress and of the Prisons-Reformation.

John Bunyan sent forth his Pilgrim 200 years ago; and 100 years afterwards John Howard, made Sheriff, accepted the burden, and beginning at this nearest jail saw the cruelties and sufferings that filled it.

In his book on the Prisons he says that he was prompted to pursue his task by the sorrows of the sufferers and love to his country. Of this book Sir Samuel Romilly said it was one of the works rare in all ages, written only for the good of mankind. A few words show one evil of many which Howard described. "In some jails," he said, "you see boys of 12 or 14 eagerly listening to the stories told by practised criminals, of their adventures, stratagems, and escapes." And, "The intention of our laws with regard to petty offenders certainly is to correct and reform them! Instead of which their confinement doth notoriously increase the vices it was designed to suppress. Multitudes of young creatures committed for some trifling offense are totally ruined there. I affirm that if it were the aim of magistrates to effect the destruction, present and future, of young delinquents, they could not devise a more effectual method than to confine them in our prisons, those seminaries of idleness and every vice."

In after years men and women of kindred spirit did much to provide for delinquent youth in England, but no law existed under which they could be taken into custody and cared for.

In 1853, eighty years after Howard began his revelations, two prize essays were printed in London for which a noble lady awarded £300. The object was to prove it the duty of society; 1, To save the young if possible from crime; 2, To save them if possible from becoming worse after its commission. They fill a handsome volume of 400 pages, and, showing the example of this House of Refuge in New York, and others that followed it in this country, and the insufficiency of mere voluntary effort, they demand the authority of law for the custody and care of juvenile delinquents, and that they be not treated as criminals to be punished, but as children to be instructed and reformed.

Precisely thus were they treated in this State under the Act of March, 1824, in this House of Refuge established by it; at whose foundation appear the names of Griscom, and Colden, and Gerard, and Stephen Allen, and Maxwell, with many others equally honored in those days; and that of the great Governor Clinton, who, in a message delivered soon afterwards, pronounced it "The best institution" for its objects, "ever devised by the wit, and established by the beneficence of man."

It was the pioneer. And first of all, it aimed at and secured control. This is as great a blessing as surprise to the subject of it. Then came the common school and daily industry, both unknown before to many, with recreation sweetened by the work in school and shop that went before or followed it. Entrance to the House brought two rules to the child which he never forgot. 1. Tell no lies. 2. Always do the best you can.

It also brought cleanliness, and clothing decent and comfortable. Food was simple and sufficient, and the dormitory was airy and well furnished; and ample provision was made for sickness by proper rooms, and medicine and attendance. Above all, and through all, prevailed the idea that God the Creator is the Govcruor of all, whose word given unto men to be their guide brings peace and safety to those who obey it, while the judgment it denounces against the unrepenting disobedient is sure to come. And little children and youth learned in the Gospel the life and lessons of the Lord their Redeemer who came to seek and to save them that were lost.

The work was indeed revolutionary, and its results and present condition have justified all that its founders claimed for it, and perhaps exceeded their hopes. In the first 20 years the earnings from labor were about 23 per cent. of the expenditures. In the next ten, 36; in the next, 30 (we were removing to this island); and in the last, 43½ per cent. Yet, industry and not gain, has been the chief object in organizing labor, and no more than a reasonable portion of time is taken for it, and it is always controlled by officers of the House, and never by contractors. Merit is sure to be recorded and commended. Fault is sure to be noted and censured. Each inmate is accounted with every week, and knows of the badge, whether standing at 1, or 2, or 3, or 4. *Four* is bad, and *one*, continued 13 weeks, promotes to the Class of Honor. Our commencement on 1st January, 1825, was in a building which had been a U. S. Arsenal, in the south part of the present Madison Square, and which was purchased with funds of the society. In 1839 the Refuge was transferred to Bellevue, at 23d street and East River, where it continued until it was brought hither in 1854. The corner-stone of this building was laid the 24th of November, 1852.

Of the Managers then in office but five are living; John A. Weeks, John W. C. Leveridge, Benj. B. Atterbury, Edgar S. Van Winkle, and Frederick W. Downer. Of the Building Committee, but one survives, Mr. Leveridge.

Beginning with three boys and six girls, there had been received on 1st January, 1875, 15,791, and there were then in the house 789, of whom 112 were girls. The expenses for 1874 were something over $121,000; of which $60,500 came from the State, $41,594 from labor of inmates; about $7,500 from the Board of Education; $7,000 from theatre licenses, and about $4,500 from a balance on hand and sales of old articles. This shows the sources of our income, and that a tax on theatres is one of them. This is especially commended by our London prize essays. And we anticipate from this source $15,000 in the present year, a litigation instituted to overthrow the law imposing the tax having proved unsuccessful. The labor has been chiefly in manufacture of hoop-skirts, wire-work and shoes; the latter the greatest. But after the recent panic the shoe contract was given up, and the work of printing has taken its place, which is very satisfactory. What has been said of labor relates to that of the boys, but it would be unjust to say nothing of the girls' labor. Our last report shows for the year about 90,000 articles made or repaired by sewing, and nearly 270,000 articles washed; all by the girls. Nor has labor brought compensation to us only. Four years ago a new plan of work was devised by which a reward for labor and good conduct was brought to the boys themselves. A class of 50 entered the "new shop," 21st January, 1871, and 32 graduated from it during the year and were honorably discharged. An account was opened with each, and a pass-book given, and written up every week. The amount thus earned by these boys during the year above the contract price was $3,904.10, paid by the contractor; and the 32 boys who graduated received $3,320.28, averaging $107.10 to each. In the following year, 1872, the work of the new shop was continued, and $4,795.13 was credited and paid to the boys, but at its close the shop was discontinued, the contractor withdrawing from it under circumstances making it necessary then; but we relinquish not the hope of a return to the plan of the "new shop."

The schools are a notable feature of our work. Surely ignorance is the parent of vice. In the last 20 years, of the 9,163 inmates received, 5,652 could not read; while of the 8,826 discharged, all could read, and 6,510 could read well. And the rapid progress from ignorance to knowledge is often surprising, well rewarding the care bestowed. A recent rule encourages the girls to aim at employment as teachers of primary classes at a moderate compensation, and one of them is now so engaged, doing very well.

And what is perceptible as results in 50 years? This: that some three-fourths of our inmates become good citizens. Men and women come hither after long absence to tell of benefits received and prosperity that followed. Fathers and mothers of Christian families who were children here, come back and tell of the past and the present; sometimes with tears of joy and thankfulness. Some, here once, take part now in making laws; others, in administering them, and all these honorably. They are found in the various occupations of life pursuing a course marked by integrity and good repute. And it should be known that some committed here were not unlettered, or the children of the obscure. Some were children of a parentage known and honored in the State. And they, too, found here a place for repentance and a way of return to virtue.

The fostering care of the Legislature has been large and continued. We gratefully remember and acknowledge its beneficence. It gave these buildings, and has given annually liberal and sufficient appropriations. And more; we owe to it laws directing towards our support certain taxes laid upon amusements before alluded to and a steady refusal to repeal them or to reduce those taxes to a nominal sum. And more, far more, we owe to the last Legislature an emphatic refusal to change fundamentally, and as we think fatally, our simple mode of life as a reformatory by subjecting it to sectarian domination; and for this, under God who has upheld us, and in view of all the benefits and blessings we have received, we are thankful to day and glad, giving unto Him the praise.

And now, our charge—our girls and boys—I turn to you with deeper interest than ever for having before this honored assembly, and before you, told the story of this House. You will never forget this day, nor the company gathered here of excellent and eminent persons full of sympathy with you, and full of hope that you may rise from adversity to an honorable and prosperous life. Therefore with this powerful incitement to effort and the sure promise of the Divine aid to all who rightly seek it, so seek that you may obtain; and then go on and prosper.

Professor Lasar then led the boys and girls in the following song, the trumpets accompanying: ·

"EIN FESTE BERG IST UNSER GOTT."

MARTIN LUTHER.

Music by J. S. BACH.

Our God stands firm a rock and tow'r,
A shield when danger presses;
A ready help in ev'ry hour,
When doubt or pain distresses!
For our malignant foe
Unswerving aims his blow;
His fearful arms the while,
Dark pow'r and darker guile;
His hidden craft is matchless.

Our strength is weakness in the fight;
Our courage soon defection;
But comes a Warrior clad in might,
A Prince of God's election!
Who is this wondrous Chief,
That brings this grand relief?
The field of battle boasts,
Christ Jesus, Lord of Hosts,
Still conq'ring and to conquer!

Then Lord arise! lift up thine arm!
With mighty succor stay us!
Oh! turn aside the deadly harm,
When Satan would betray us;
That rescued by Thy hand,
In triumph we may stand,
And 'round Thy footstool crowd
In joy to sing aloud
High praise to our Redeemer!

The President then introduced to the audience the Rev. Doctor John Hall, who spoke, as follows.

Ladies and Gentlemen :

I may be allowed to begin by expressing the great satisfaction which I feel in being permitted to take any part in these your Anniversary Exercises—exercises that have this peculiarity about them, that they review fifty years of diligent, honest, industrious, and by the blessing of God, very successful labors, in the cause of true and enlightened humanity. If I rightly understand the purposes for which I am here, it is to utter a few words to the encouragement of the friends who compose this Society, and who have been, with zeal and without selfishness, the supporters of this great effort; diligent co-operators in this patriotic Christian work; and moreover to express the regard that is and ought to be felt for it by the general public, and which I think will be cherished for it the more, the more attention is given to the subject.

I shall not permit myself to forget, that we do not meet here as of any section or class, religiously or politically. We have met here in the character of American citizens—may I not say of American Christian citizens?—that we may see what has been done, that we may learn what benefits have been conferred, with a view to greater efficiency, and that we may stimulate and encourage one another in what is undoubtedly a labor of love.

There is one drawback to the satisfaction that I feel in standing here to speak a few words from this place, namely, that I have no special adaptation to an occasion of this kind. Yet it may be alleged that I have a general adaptation. That seems to me to lie in two principal things which come to any mind. The first is, that I am a clergyman. I belong to a class of men in definite relation to sympathy with and co-oper- ation in all beneficence.

That is true of the clergymen in every denomination. I do not claim too much for my order, when I say that there are nowhere in the community more practical sympathetic energy than among the class to which I belong. Our Master said, "Go and sin no more." And it would be shame to us, if we were lacking in sympathy and in the spirit of ready co-operation with every agency and in every institution designed to win men from vice to virtue.

The other adaptation to which I allude is totally diff- erent in character, for, Mr. President, I belong to that portion of the population which I am sorry to say makes the largest contribution of inmates of this institution, namely, the children of foreign birth. I come under that description. I am sorry to say that the per- centage of the foreign born coming into this Institution, as compared with the children of the native American, has steadily and uniformly risen to 86 and 87 per cent., as appears from your records. Nor can I fail to own the generosity with which the country charges itself with the care of so many who have not the claim of birth-right.

I came from that Island which is capable of produc- ing so much, which within the last year has supplied more than half of all the inmates of this institution. I am an Irish boy, very well grown as you see, but an Irish boy nevertheless. I should like to ask this question, which I often ask myself: Had I been placed in less happy circumstances, had I been without parents to care and provide for me, had I been thrown among the corrupt and corrupting, what evidence is there that I would not have been much in the same condition, and in need of the same Christian help, which is extended in this place to so many who have come from that same Island? I am profoundly sorry that that Island sends hither so many of its youthful population. I am profoundly sorry that this acknowledgment has to be made by me in the beginning of this statement.

These two points may be dwelt upon with some satisfaction. In the first place, the large-heartedness and great-mindedness of this American people, exhibited by giving home comforts to such large proportions of strangers of one country or another, which have been thrown as a burden upon the community, a burden it seems to me taken up and carried with the least possible murmuring and the least possible complaint. That is something to the highest possible credit of the American people, and which ought to be acknowledged.

The second circumstance that deserves notice is the proportion of the ignorant that come to this institution, which seems amply to provide for their instruction, so that the next generation and the succeeding generation will be better as citizens; better as Christian people, better as members of the community than its predecessor, and so on in all time. This is something for which, it seems to me, we ought to be thankful and ought to lift our hearts, full of hope and gratitude, to Almighty God.

Mr. President, it might be supposed that there must be a steady and alarming increase of ignorance, vice,

and crime in the community, seeing that such masses
of this ignorance, vice, and crime are presented to you
from time to time in recent years; but I think you will
see upon second thought that such a supposition is a
mistake. It is true indeed that with the growth of great
cities there must be an inevitable growth of the classes
sometimes called dangerous. It is a fact that great
cities make the largest contributions to institutions of
this kind. You will see from the statistics that the
City of New York and its sister cities that are growing
around it send an overwhelming mass of children, while
the rural counties of the State that have not any large
towns, or even considerable villages, are hardly repre-
sented at all in the contribution of inmates to this place.
With the growth of great cities among us, we must
have and expect poverty, vice, and suffering, that will
make demand upon the Christian feeling of the community.

But it is ever to be borne in mind that the greater seem-
ing increase of vice and crime is due less to a real increase of these, than to the better means of knowledge
that we have now than we formerly possessed. We are
registering and reporting these evils more than we used
to do in former times. Their history is served up in a
newspaper at our breakfast table; we see a long col-
umn of crimes, and naturally think the world must be
growing worse; but the fact is, that the present is a
thousand times better than the past, and while the tre-
mendous list of crime is shown to the world in these reports, whose eyes rest upon the gentle deeds of beneficence, done in modest quiet, side by side with them?
There is every reason for the encouragement of the
friends of this institution, and perhaps, if you please.

the grounds of this encouragement may be stated with advantage to those who are present.

In the first place, it is something upon which you, ladies and gentlemen, may be well congratulated, that there are upon this island such commodious and proper buildings for the carrying on of this work. I have been taken through them, some of them more than once. I have had opportunity before of speaking from this desk, and I have a tolerably definite idea of the character of this entire structure, and for what purposes it has been called into existence nearly 25 years; it is particularly worthy of praise for the freeness with which the atmos-, phere circulates through it, and for the abundance of light that it enjoys. We remember that it was said in the beginning "let there be light, and there was light," and it was also said, "and the light was good," which may be said of this place. Nor can one fail to be struck with the beauty of the surroundings. Many persons in the city are now in quest of just such shade and flowers It seems to me it would not be a bad idea for us to come hither also.

I have been looking over the names of those who have been Presidents, Vice-Presidents and Managers of this Institution for the last half century. I have been struck with the fact that so many of them are well known in New York, names that are always mentioned with respect, and that have commanded the most perfect confidence of the people. That is an honorable roll of gentlemen dead and living, who have been the steady friends of this institution, dead some of them, as far as this life is concerned—dead as far as we can see, but living still in precious memory—living still in the institution they helped to found. I was doubly interested

as I came and landed upon this Island, when in the first
person I met I recognized a young man whose father,
twenty years ago, presided over you. I was glad to see
him here taking his place among the managers of this
institution, the trust of beneficence and kindness coming down from father to son. What nobler heritage
than that could be bestowed upon any man?

Some of these managers I have the great pleasure to
know personally. Of the living I shall not speak, but of
the dead, whom I knew, I may speak a few words. I
recall the late Mr. McMartin, who took an active part
in this work. I remember his kindness of heart, his
quiet humor, his never-failing good temper, his keen
sagacity, and that large beneficence that marked him a
Christian. I remember seeing him for the last time at
Belfast, in the North of Ireland. He was in the most
joyous spirits, looking back with gratitude, looking for-
ward with hope. It pleased God a few months after
this, that his eventful life should be brought to an end
in a foreign land. I say now to you, gentlemen, in view
of his departure, "Work while it is day, for the night
cometh, when no man can work."

I also had the privilege of knowing the late Mr. Oliver S. Strong. It was my duty to visit him in his sickness in the city, when he had no expectation of ever being well again. I remember his gentlemanly bearing,
his fine temper, his great tenderness of heart, and his
strong faith was evidenced by the calmness with which
he saw the near approach of death.

I take it that these men are specimens of the dead
and of the living who were entrusted with the care of
this institution. It has thus a noble history, and because of this noble history it may well claim the confi-

dence of Christian people of the present and of the future. Half a century is a long time in the history of an institution, and when we remember the sharp and vigilant eye that has been kept over the men governing this institution, and that it has stood the test for half a century, we must feel that it is not to be tampered with lightly; it is not to be touched with hasty hands, nor should any of its methods be dispensed with until some reasonable assurance has been given to the community that one better and more thorough can be put in its stead.

As far back as 1788, some excellent people in London came to look with great pain and sorrow upon the wretched condition of the juvenile criminal of the metropolis; and they tried to have something done in their behalf. They grouped the children in families of twelve each in cottages in the Village of Harkney, placing a tailor, gardener or shoemaker at the head of each and making his wife a kind of housemother to the family. Later, in the year 1818, in Warwickshire in England, the effort was made, but died out with its founder. In 1830, England produced a man, Captain Brenton, who took this matter up with a clear head and warm heart. He came to the conclusion that it was criminal to put young children among older prisoners who related their crimes and spread corruption Reformatory agencies he connected with schools and sought the aid of Parliament, but failed in his efforts. But a noble woman, noble in rank and title, noble in feeling and spirit, took the matter in hand and founded the Victoria Asylum for girls. Large numbers of boys were sent to the Colonies at the Cape of Good Hope. Many believed they were sold as slaves to the Dutch.

Look at these boys at my right hand; look at these
on my left and see the intelligence expressed in their
faces. It is here that you can give them direction in
which they should go. When they have gone from
your control, all hope of their improvement is also gone.
It is a good thing that you get the children while young.
I bespeak your pity for them. Many of them knew not
much of the love of a mother. . . . .
Many of them knew not much of the sweetness of a
pure home.

And I think I may add, as a final statement in this
connection, that this Institution has produced noble results in every aspect.

I have been figuring up from the statistics, the amount
of money that has been invested during this half century in this Institution. I make it out to be about
$ 2,100,000 for maintenance, and $750,000, or three
quarters of a million for the buildings and all the repairs
that have been effected upon them ; that is to say, under
three millions of dollars have sufficed to do all this work
during this half century. Three million dollars of
money ! That seems a good deal of money, I presume,
to the most of these boys. It is a good deal to most of
us ministers, who are not accustomed to deal with so
much, except in figures. But there are merchants who
would take their breakfasts just as comfortably if they
had given three millions to build a house or bridge or a
canal or a railroad, they would not lose the employments
that are necessary for their welfare. A well arranged
"ring" could manage to extract three millions in two or
three years.

The point that I want to make—and I am glad to see
that the boys understand it—that this work has been

done for fifty years most cheaply and I should like to know where in this community can three millions be pointed out that have produced better and nobler and more substantial results than these. Three millions of money, for which between fifteen and sixteen thousand human beings with capacity for love and hatred, with capacity for joys and sorrows, have received benefits that have torn them from crime and woe and sent them out a blessing to their country. Between fifteen and sixteen thousand have had a chance to get an education, have had a chance to become good women and men, true citizens and Christians. I shall be glad to know where so much has been done for the benefit of so many with the paltry sum of three millions of money.

But then it is to be borne in mind that, if I am not mistaken in my reading, some of the money has been earned here. This present year represents something like 40 per cent. so earned. So that, even while saying three millions, I might as well have said two, because of this 25 or 30 or 40 per cent. was earned by the boys and girls. This represents education, diligence, painstaking, and indefinite capacity on the part of the boys and girls to earn their bread at some future time.

In the best of books we read of Paradise where our first parents were placed. There were four things given to man in his condition of happiness. There were laws defining good from evil; there was the Sabbath which was to be kept holy. There was the work to be done to till the ground and keep it. The first thing that God gave to man in the garden was a happy home, when he put husband and wife together and there founded the first household. If you want to make your life happy, it is necessary to have work for brain and muscle, a Sabbath rightly kept, the sweetness and purity of a happy home, and obedience to law; and children, remember that these things are possible for you.

Jesus is the Son of God to whom all things are possible. Go to Him. He can give to you all you need, if you but let him. Remember when here on earth they brought little children to him and he laid his hands on them and blessed them. If you go to him he will lay his hands upon you and he will bless you. All will be well in time—all will be well with you when time is no more. May God bless you, boys and girls, and fit you to be a blessing to the world.

The children afterward sang, led as before, the following song:

"THE EVERLASTING MEMORIAL."

BY DR. HORATIUS BONAR.

Music from "*Sacred Crown*," of Boston

Up and away like the dew of the morning,
   Soaring from earth to its home in the sun,
So let me steal away gently and lovingly,
   Only remembered by what I have done.

Up and away like the odors of sunset,
   Sweetening the twilight as darkness comes on,
So be my life, a thing felt but unnoticed,
   And I but remembered by what I have done.

My name and my place and my tomb all forgotten,
   The brief race of time well and patiently run,
So let me pass away peacefully, silently,
   Only remembered by what I have done.

So let my living be, so be my dying,
   So let my name lie unblazoned, unknown,
Upraised and unmissed, I shall still be remembered,
   Yes—but remembered by what I have done.

The President then read before the audience the letter which, in fulfilment of his promise, was written by Ex-Governor Seymour. It is as follows:

LETTER FROM EX-GOVERNOR HON. HORATIO SEYMOUR.

Utica, May 31, 1875.

To

Edgar Ketchum, Esq.,

President of the New York House of Refuge.

Sir:—I am sorry I cannot attend the Fiftieth Anniversary of your society, as I wish to show my interest in that institution, and my respect for its managers. It has been my painful duty to act upon thousands of prayers for pardon, and to study with care, the sources and history of crime. Beyond most men, I have had opportunities for seeing the great value of the work of "The Society for the Reformation of Juvenile Delinquents." I will not dwell upon its direct charities. It has, beyond these, a wide influence in teaching our people and their legislators the causes and courses of wrong doing. It is among youthful offenders, where the earliest influences which shape character are most clearly seen, that the great truth that crime is the outgrowth of social condition, is exhibited in the clearest light, and that the public as well as the offender, is involved in its guilt. There never was an indictment found against a man which was not in some degree, an indictment of the community in which he lived. Criminals are representative men.

They are not exceptional men who run against the current of society, but they float with them and into crime, because they do not resist the influences which drift them into wrong doing. One of the great truths which must be stamped upon the public mind is, that the inmates of prisons are not men unlike ourselves, but they are ourselves, under other circumstances, and we must take care that the circumstances tend to promote virtue and not to foster vice. My experience with men of all conditions leads me to feel kindly toward those who err, and to believe that there is in all some good upon which we can base hopes of reform.

The best minds of our own and of other countries are now studying the courses of crime and the cures for its baleful work. As it is analyzed, the conviction grows that States must not only have wise penal codes, that they must not merely try to reform wrong doers, but that above all, that the existence of crime in any community is proof of the guilt of the whole community. In no other penal establishments are these great truths so clearly seen and so deeply felt as in those designed for the care and instruction of juvenile delinquents. The people of New York are not only indebted to the managers of the House of Refuge for their work of charity for the children under their care, but they are still more indebted to them for making clear the duty of every citizen to exert himself in the extirpation of vice, the reformation of offenders, and the elevation of the whole community to higher planes of virtue and intelligence

I am truly yours, &c.,

HORATIO SEYMOUR.

Then again the children sang, led as before, the following hymn. ·

"ABIDE WITH ME."

BY REV. H. F. LYTE.

Music from "The Hymnary" of S. Lasar.

Abide with me ! Fast falls the eventide ;
  The darkness deepens, Lord with me abide!
When other helpers fail, and comforts flee,
  Help of the helpless, O abide with me !

Come not in terrors, as the King of kings,
  But kind and good, with healing in thy wings;
Tears for all woes, a heart for every plea ;
  Come, Friend of sinners, thus abide with me ;

Thou on my head in early youth didst smile ;
  And though rebellious and perverse meanwhile,
Thou hast not left me oft as I left thee ;
  On to the close, O Lord abide with me !

I need Thy presence ev'ry passing hour,
  What but Thy grace can foil the tempter's pow'r,
Who like Thyself my guide and stay can be ?
  Through cloud and sunshine, O abide with me !

These exercises were spread over the two sessions of morning and afternoon, at the end of which the Rev. E D. Murphy pronounced the benediction. And there were interspersed some fine pieces of music sung by a quartette composed of the Misses Clementina and Agnes Lasar, and Messrs. F. Crane and C. A. McPherson, who were accompanied on the piano by Prof. S. Lasar.

At noon, also, there was served in the dining-room of the boys' second division, a collation, the Rev. Dr. C. D. Foss asking the Divine blessing.

During the day the visitors had opportunity, which was generally improved, to inspect the dormitories, school-rooms, work-shops, kitchen, bake-shop, dining-room, play-grounds, bath-rooms and offices.

TABLE SHOWING THE ADMISSIONS AND DISCHARGES, AND OTHER STATISTICS DURING EACH DECADE, FROM 1825 TO 1875.

	1st Decade. 1825 to 1835.		2d Decade. 1835 to 1845.		3d Decade. 1845 to 1855.		4th Decade. 1855 to 1865.		5th Decade. 1865 to 1875.	
	Whole Number Committed 1,678.	Per Cent.	Whole Number Committed 1,858.	Per Cent.	Whole Number Committed 3,101.	Per Cent.	Whole Number Committed 3,490.	Per Cent.	Whole Number Committed 5.664.	Per Cent.
Males	1,261	75	1,304	70	2,508	81	2,709	78	4,763	84
Females	417	25	554	30	593	19	781	22	901	16
Native parents	740	44	643	34½	674	22	498	14	771	13 6-10
Foreign parents	938	56	1,215	65½	2,427	78	2,992	86	4,893	86 4-4
Could read	1,090	65	1,047	56	1,691	54½	745	21½	1,136	20
Could not read	598	35	811	44	1,410	45½	2,745	78½	4,528	80
Criminal	904	54	882	47½	1,866	60	2,145	62	3,212	57
Vagrant and truant	774	46	976	52½	1,235	40	1,345	38	2,452	43
Were returned	249	15	311	16½	583	19	547	15½	653	11
Under ten years of age	130	8	98	5	95	3	69	2	224	4
From ten to fourteen years	693	41	735	39½	1,151	37	1,196	34	1,787	31
From fourteen to sixteen years	591	35	723	39	1,294	43	1,439	41	2,106	37
Sixteen years and more	264	16	302	16½	561	18	786	23	1,547	28
Were indentured	1,160	70	1,523	82	2,486	80	1,905	55	1,217	26
Were discharged	195	11	186	10	409	13½	1,349	39	3,571	72½
Were enlisted	254	15	72	4	141	4½	185	5	3	......
Escaped	45	2½	57	3	33	1	24	½	25	½
Died	24	1½	20	1	32	1	27	½	59	1
RESULTS.									*	
Favorable	792	47	702	37	1,189	38½	988	29	568	12
Unfavorable	273	17	198	10½	616	20	319	9	206	4
Unknown	589	36	938	52½	1,264	41½	2,156	62	4,101	84

* 4,875 discharged.

TABLE XII, SHOWING STATISTICS OF THOSE HEARD FROM FAVORABLY DURING THE FIVE DECADES.

	1st Decade. 1825 to 1835.		2d Decade. 1835 to 1845.		3d Decade. 1845 to 1855.		4th Decade. 1855 to 1865.		5th Decade. 1865 to 1875.	
	Whole No. 792.	Per ce't	Whole No. 702.	Per ce't.	Whole No. 1,189.	Per ce't.	Whole No. 988.	Per ce't.	Whole No.	Per ce't.
Males	579	74	450	64	919	77	716	72½		
Females	213	25	252	36	270	23	272	27½		
Native parents	335	42	231	33	286	24	165	17		
Foreign parents	457	58	471	67	903	76	823	83		
Could read	535	67	406	58	628	53	193	20		
Could not read	257	32	296	42	561	47	795	80		
Criminal	419	53	299	42	658	55	628	63½		
Vagrant and truant	373	47	403	58	531	45	360	36½		
Under 10 years of age	57	7	42	6	52	4½	44	4½		
From 10 to 14 years	339	42½	296	42	509	43	365	36½		
From 14 to 16 years	274	34½	275	39	458	38½	375	38		
16 years and more	124	16	89	13	170	14	204	21		
Were indentured	634	81	656	93½	1,024	86	703	74		
" discharged	49	6	24	3½	119	10	189	19		
" enlisted	109	13	22	3	46	4	66	7		

The following financial statement is for fifty years, divided into five decades.

The cost for real estate and buildings for the use of the Institution, including repairs and improvements, was as follows:

1st Decade	1825 to 1835	$78,740 80
2d "	1835 to 1845	61,432 98
3d "	1845 to 1855	204,133 12
4th	1855 to 1865	273,688 81
5th "	1865 to 1875	127,744 60
Total for fifty years		$745,740 31

This amount was paid in part by private subscriptions and donations, and the remainder by money received for insurance for loss by fires, money received from sale of property in Twenty-third street, New York, and by State appropriations.

The amount of private subscriptions and donations was (the former), $31,702.04 (the latter), legacies for Library Fund, $7,000—total, $38,702.04.

The present value of the real estate and buildings is more than the whole cost and outlay; therefore, nothing is charged against the Institution on this account.

The property 37½ acres of land and buildings, is entirely free from incumbrance.

The cost for support, which includes every item of expense except for grounds and buildings, was as follows:

						Amount.
1st Decade—number inmates, including returned,					1,927....	$130,233 26
2d " " " " "					2,169....	147,916 04
3d " " " " "					3,684....	238,378 74
4th " " "					4,037....	527,463 81
5th " " " " "					6,317....	1,062,017 31
Total expense for support						$2,106,009 16

The above expense was paid from moneys received from appropriations made by the State and by the City of New York, from the licenses of theatres, from the excise and marine funds, from the sale of articles not needed for the use of the Institution, such as old barrels, rags, iron, &c., and from the earnings by the inmates.

From the two latter sources the following amounts were received:

	Articles Sold.	Earnings.	Total.
1st Decade........	$68 67	$29,526 84	$29,595 51
2d "	587 08	33,984 43	34,571 51
3d "	2,072 50	83,974 41	86,046 91
4th	3,546 11	154,275 35	157,821 46
5th	14,027 35	445,126 57	459,153 92
	$20,301 71	$746,887 60	$767,189 31

This amount deducted from the whole cost for support, the balance shows the net cost.

	Whole Cost.	Earnings, &c.	Net Cost.
1st Decade........	$130,233 26	$29,595 51	$100,637 75
2d "	147,916 04	34,571 51	113,344 53
3d "	238,378 74	86,046 91	152,331 83
4th	527,463 81	157,821 46	369,642 35
5th	1,062,017 31	459,153 92	602,863 39
	$2,106,009 16	$767,189 31	$1,338,819 85

The following shows the percentage of the cost of support paid by the earnings and the articles sold:

1st Decade	....	22⅔	per cent.
2d "	....	23¼	"
3d "	....	36 1.10	"
4th	....	30	
5th ..	....	43 3.10	..

The less amount in the 4th decade was occasioned by the interruption of the labor in consequence of the removal of the Institution from 23d street, N. Y., to its present location and by the financial crisis of 1857.

In the first report of the Board of Managers, made after one year of experience (January 1, 1826), speaking of the support of the children of the Institution, they say: "When the Institution is well organized, it is the belief of Managers that the profits of their labor will cover a considerable portion of the expense of their maintenance." This idea has never been lost to view; and although the introduction of labor into the House has been always considered of importance primarily as a reformatory process, yet the profits coming from it have never been lightly esteemed. No more work is exacted than is healthful and beneficial to the inmates.

RULES OF THE NEW YORK HOUSE OF REFUGE.

GENERAL RULES.

1. TELL NO LIES.
2. ALWAYS DO THE BEST YOU CAN.

RULES FOR THE ENFORCEMENT OF DISCIPLINE.

I. The boys and girls are divided into four grades, according to conduct.

GRADE 1 includes the best behaved and most orderly boys and girls; those who do not lie nor use profane language; who are neat and tidy in their persons and cleanly in their habits; who do not willfully or carelessly waste, injure, or destroy property belonging to the House, and who are always respectful to the officers.

GRADE 2 embraces those who are fair in conduct, but not entirely free from the faults mentioned above.

GRADE 3 consists of those whose conduct is not so good as those in Grade 2. The first grade of a boy is always 3.

GRADE 4 is the lowest, and one of disgrace; it is only given in cases of continued or gross misconduct. A former inmate, returned for fault, is placed in Grade 4.

II. For violation of rules, boys and girls are degraded from 1 to 2, from 2 to 3, and from 3 to 4; for improvement in conduct they are raised in grade from 4 to 3, and from 3 to 2, and 2 to 1. Any boy or girl continuing for thirteen weeks in succession in Grade 1, is advanced to the Class of Honor, and wears an appropriate badge.

III. The grades are determined every Saturday evening, in the presence of the whole Division, according to the marks made during the week.

IV. Five marks, lower the grade one step; four leave it the same as the previous week; less than four are forgiven.

V. In the Second Division, punishment with the strap degrades to 4, except when the subject is in the Class of Honor, in which case it degrades to 2.

VI. Boys and girls gain their release from the Refuge by retaining Grade 1 for fifty-two weeks in succession, and by attaining to the highest class in school; and they are discharged from the House when a proper place is provided for them.

VII. No applications from parents or friends of children will be entertained by the Indenturing Committee until the inmate applied for shall have been in Grade 1 at least six weeks next preceding the time of application, and shall have reached at least the third class in school.

VIII. When an inmate has been degraded to 4, an addition of two weeks' continuance in Grade 1, required by the foregoing rule, will be made before an application for discharge can be heard; and one week more is added for every other grade of 4 received.

IX. Grades can be changed only by the Assistant Superintendent, in case of boys, and by the Matron in case of girls, for offenses committed out of school; and by the Principal for offenses occurring in school.

X. Any officer in charge of boys or girls may give, for disorderly conduct, not to exceed two marks during any one week, provided the marks given, added to those already imposed by others during the same week, do not exceed four.

XI. Before any marks are given, the boy or girl must be required to tell the number of marks already received, and the statement must be taken and noted.

XII. In case an inmate makes a false statement, which will be discovered at "Badge call," the offender shall be degraded at least two grades, or may be punished according to the discretion of the officer in charge. In the latter case, the grade will be 4.

XIII. When the aggregate marks for the week amount to four, and other offenses are counted, the boys out of school must be reported to the Assistant Superintendent, and the girls to the Matron; and all cases in school, either boys or girls, must be reported to the Principal. After a report is made to the Assistant Superintendent, Matron, or Principal, no marks can be altered or canceled, except by their approval; nor can these officers cancel any marks legitimately given by the subordinate officers previous to the report.

XIV. When the grade is determined at the calling of the badges at the close of the week, it cannot be changed, except by the consent of the Superintendent.

DESCRIPTION OF THE BUILDINGS.

The House of Refuge is located on the easterly Bank of the Harlem River, on Randall's Island, and directly opposite that portion of the City of New York which is included between One Hundred and Fifteenth and One hundred and Twentieth streets. The buildings are of brick, erected in the Italian style. The two principal structures front the river, and form a façade nearly a thousand feet in length. The line of their fronts is exactly parallel with the city avenues. The larger of the two buildings is for the accommodation of the boys' department, the other for the girls'. Other buildings are located in the rear of these, and are inclosed by a stone wall twenty feet high. A division wall, of like height, separates the grounds of the boys' department from that of the girls', and in each department walls separate the inmates into two divisions.

The boys' house is nearly six hundred feet long. The dome-surmounted portions are devoted to the use of the officers; the central mass also contains the chapel; while the extreme portions contain the hospitals and lavatories. There are six hundred and thirty-six dromitories, five feet by seven and seven feet high, in the portion between the center and the end buildings. In the rear is the school and dining-hall building seventy by one hundred and thirty-eight feet. A central brick wall divides the building in each story into two equal parts, one for each division. The lower story is appropriated to dining-rooms and the upper story to school-rooms. In the rear of the school building, are the kitchen and bakery, occupying a space twenty-five by ninety feet. The workshops are at the northerly and southerly extremities of the yard, and are each thirty by one hundred feet, and three stories high.

The girls' house is two hundred and fifty feet long, the central portion of which contains the apartments of the matron, assistants, and female teachers, while the wings contain two hundred and fifty dormitories for the inmates. In the rear, connected by two corridors or covered halls, is a building for school-rooms and dining-halls, the hospitals, sewing-rooms, and lavatories being at each end, with the laundry in the rear.

The whole establishment is supplied with Croton water, brought across the Harlem River in a three and one quarter inch lead pipe. Tanks are in the attics of the principal buildings, and a reservoir of one hundred feet diameter, located beyond the inclosure, affords a reserve for extraordinary occasions, as well as a plentiful supply of ice in the winter.

CIRCULAR TO PARENTS AND GUARDIANS.

SOCIETY FOR THE

REFORMATION OF JUVENILE DELINQUENTS,

HOUSE OF REFUGE. (*Randall's Island*).

..............187....

The Managers of the House of Refuge take this method of informing you that.........your........has been received as an inmate of their Institution, to remain during minority, or until discharged by the Managers or by due process of law.

For your information, the Managers deem it proper to state that the Institution is not a place of punishment, nor a prison, but a Reform School where the inmates receive such instruction and training as are best adapted to form and perpetuate a virtuous character; to establish habits of industry, and to advance them in those branches of knowledge which are taught in the Common Schools of the State.

They are accordingly provided with a home every way pleasant and comfortable; are furnished with steady employment of a kind to enable them to earn their own support after their discharge; have appropriate seasons of recreation; are well fed and clothed, and, when sick, are attended by the House Physician and carefully nursed; are regularly gathered into school at certain hours on five days of the week, and on the Sabbath are furnished with suitable religious and moral instructions. In order to accomplish the wise ends contemplated by the beneficent provision of the State, the inmates must remain a sufficient time to receive such training and discipline as will serve to reform their evil habits, and to establish in them correct principles and habits of industry. The Managers, therefore, are guided in their decisions as to the term during which inmates shall be retained in the House by their conduct while confined, and, with a due regard to the previous history of the inmate, either prolong or shorten the period of confinement, according to the circumstances of greater or less delinquency in each case. Applications for the discharge of inmates are frequently made within a few weeks after their commitment, which, however, cannot be entertained. Only in special cases, the circumstances of which can be stated at the City Office, will applications be received by the Indenturing Committee under twelve months from the date of committal.

Parents, guardians, and other near friends of those children sent from the Cities of New York and Brooklyn, are permitted to visit them once in a month, and on their first visit will receive a card designating these periods. Where friends reside at a distance from the city, they will be permitted to see their children at any time they are in the city, provided their visits are not oftener than once in a month. If unable from residing at too great a distance, to visit their children, they will be permitted to write to them once within the prescribed period, and to receive letters in return.

In case of the serious illness of any child, the friends will at once be advised of its condition.

The House of Refuge is on Randall's Island, in the Twelfth Ward of the City of New York, and the ferry at the foot of East One Hundred and Nineteenth street can be reached at all hours, either by the Second or Third Avenue Railroads, and by steamboat from Peck Slip or Fulton Slip, N. Y. The City Office is at Bennett Building, fifth floor, Room 9, corner Nassau and Fulton street, and is open between the hours 9 A. M. and 4 P. M., where the relatives and friends of children can procure information respecting their welfare.

In behalf of the Managers,

EDGAR KETCHUM, *President.*

ANDREW WARNER, *Secretary.*

Lightning Source UK Ltd.
Milton Keynes UK
UKHW012021021218
333216UK00014B/2323/P

9 780260 154736